No Walls of Stone

No Walls of Stone

❖

*An Anthology of
Literature by
Deaf and
Hard of Hearing Writers*

❖

*Jill Jepson,
Editor*

GALLAUDET UNIVERSITY PRESS
WASHINGTON, D.C.

Credits: Quote on p. 215 from *Teaching a Stone to Talk* by Annie Dillard, ©1982 by Annie Dillard, published by HarperCollins Publishers. Quote on p. 216 first published in *The Reporter,* January 26, 1967; reprinted from *The Way to Rainy Mountain* by N. Scott Momaday, ©1969, The University of New Mexico Press. Quote on p. 227 from *The Expression of the Emotions in Man and Animals* by Charles Darwin, ©1965, The University of Chicago Press. Quote on p. 229 from *In Silence* by Ruth Sidransky, ©1990 by Ruth Sidransky, published by St. Martin's Press. Quotes on pp. 230-231 from *Life at My Fingertips* by Robert J. Smithdas, ©1958, Doubleday & Co.

Excerpts from *Deafness* on pp. 146–159 reprinted by permission of the publisher from *Deafness* by David Wright, pp. 3–4, 5–7, 8–12, 49–52, © 1969 by David Wright, published by Stein and Day.

"Learning to Speak I," "Mrs. Kichak's Plum Tree," "Practice," "The Audiologist," "A Wish Unheard," and "The Finer Things" ©1992 by Raymond Luczak. Published by permission of the author.

Cover and interior photographs by Willy Conley.
Cover and interior design by Kathleen Cunningham.

Gallaudet University Press
Washington, DC 20002

Library of Congress Cataloging-in-Publication Data
No walls of stone: an anthology of literature by deaf and hard of hearing
writers/Jill Jepson, editor.
        p.   cm.
ISBN 1-56368-019-X
1. Deaf, Writings of the, American. 2. Hearing impaired, Writings of the,
American. 3. Hearing impaired—United States—Literary collections. 4. Deaf—
United States—Literary collections. 5. American literature—20th century. I.
Jepson, Jill Christine, 1950-
PS508.D43N6   1992   92-31943
810.8'09208162—dc20   CIP

The paper used in this publication meets the minimum requirements of American National Standard for Information Sciences—Permanence of Paper for Printed Library Materials, ANSI Z39.48-1984.

Contents

Introduction   1
Acknowledgments   15

Claire Blatchford

The Deaf Girl: A Memory   20
The Collector   21
Centering   23
Acorn   24
Mid-Winter   25

Robert F. Panara

On His Deafness   27
The Deaf Experience   28
Lip Service   29

Anne McDonald

For Stanley Teaching Sign Language and Us   31
The Deadening of October   33
Foxglove (for Don)   34
Wing Biddlebaum   35
Speaking About the Deaf Child   36

Willy Conley

One Frame per Second   38
The Seawall   39
The Hearing Test   46

Lisa Fay

Albert Einstein   73
My Yankee Friend   74
Subway Conductor   76

Raymond Luczak

Learning to Speak I   78
Mrs. Kichak's Plum Tree   82
The Audiologist   83
Practice   84
A Wish, Unheard   88
The Finer Things   89

Michael Winters

Melusine   114

Trudy Drucker

Sylvia   124
At Night   125
Twilight Time   127
The Fifth Voyage   128

Curtis Robbins

Piano   130
The Big Black Beetle   131
Homeless   132

Mary Holmes

Inner Ears   134

Edna Shipley-Conner

On My Impending Deafness   141
The Search   142
Oklahoma   143

David Wright

By the Effigy of St. Cecilia   145
Dialogue of a Deaf Man   146
Selections from Deafness   148

Cynthia Amerman

Aeaea   *161*
Game of Hide-and-Seek   *163*
Woodville   *164*
Birth   *165*
Medusa   *166*

Karin Mango

To Your Health   *168*
Christmas Cheer   *171*

Eddie Swayze

A Statue of Virgin Mary   *177*

Emily Mandelbaum

Skiing in January 1991   *179*
Sounds   *180*

Jack Clemo

Helen Keller at Wrentham   *182*
Affirmative Way   *184*
Whispers   *187*
Beethoven   *189*

Frances M. Parsons

Selections from I Didn't Hear
the Dragon Roar   *192*

Delores Goodrick Beggs

Tinnitus   *199*

Christopher Heuer

Larynx   *201*
Howling at the Moon   *203*
Spiraling into Sleep   *204*

Contents
vii

Joseph Castronovo
Statues   206
*Above the Entrance to an
Ancient Italian Cemetery, A Sign   209*

Peter Cook
Maltz   211
Ringoes   212

Hannah Merker
Selections from Listening   *215*

Introduction

Anthropologist Edward Hall has described literature as a rich and yet untapped source of information about how people perceive the world. My interest in collecting the writings of deaf and hard of hearing people stemmed, in part, from my belief that literature could serve as a doorway into the world of deafness. The resulting anthology, *No Walls of Stone*, provides exactly what I had hoped for—a glimpse into the perceptions, experiences, and ideas of people living with deafness or hearing loss.

For readers who are unfamiliar with the *deaf experience*, this anthology provides a unique introduction. This collection is distinct because it is written not by scholars using the analytic methods of the social sciences, but by artists who know deafness or hearing loss from first-hand experience. For all readers, this anthology presents a sampling of the remarkable works currently being produced by deaf and hard of hearing writers, as well as a small taste of exceptional earlier writings. The selections include the work of poets, novelists, short-story writers, playwrights, journalists, and essayists.

The creation of *No Walls of Stone* has been a long and complicated process, one that has aroused considerable curiosity among my colleagues. My co-workers have frequently asked me how a linguist and anthropologist, who until recently was doing research on exotic cultures in other parts of the world, came to edit an anthology of fiction by deaf and hard of hearing writers. Many factors lead me into deaf studies and, ultimately, to collecting these writings. My own (moderate) hearing loss may have been one factor; my earlier studies in a department of speech pathology and audiology probably played some role; however, the chief reason lies in my convictions about the purpose of anthropological research.

Anthropology and linguistics, the two fields in which I am trained, are disciplines that seek to understand the various ways of being in the world. Anthropologists, whether they visit Buddhist monasteries in the Himalayas, interview Russian artists, or film manioc cultivators in the Amazon, strive to comprehend the vast array of life experiences found among human beings. For many anthropologists, the study of the way people live rests on two convictions: First, that it is essential, especially now at the close of the twentieth century, for human beings to understand, accept, and interact with each other; and second, that these explorations can enable us to find the common core of human life, that level of experience shared by all human beings, regardless of the circumstances in which they live.

This interest in the diversity of human experience generally leads anthropologists to exotic cultures. After several years of living in and researching a variety of regions, however, I became interested in learning more about people in my own country whose life experiences differed significantly from the "mainstream."

Historically, deaf people have been one of the most disenfranchised groups. The history of deaf people is one of stigma, marginalization, and domination by the hearing world. Nonetheless, the achievements of deaf people have been remarkable. In recent years, the Deaf community has experienced a surge of pride and unity, while hearing people have demonstrated a growing interest in deafness. These developments have been spurred by an increased assertion by members of the Deaf community of their right to live life not as "impaired" hearing people, but as deaf people. This conviction—that deafness is not a lesser or worse condition than hearing, but a different way of being in the world—attracted me to deaf studies.

In my study of deafness, I sought answers to many questions: How do the life experiences of deaf and hearing people differ? What does it mean to be a deaf person in a predominantly hearing society? What is it like to communicate by vision rather than by sound? What types of life choices do deaf and hard of hearing people confront and how do they make those choices?

Most people discover early in their explorations that the issues raised by these questions are immensely complex. The experience of being deaf or hard of hearing is far from monolithic. The people I worked with and came to know as friends were a diverse group. Some had been deaf since birth or early childhood and some had lost their hearing as adolescents, as young adults, or in old age. They included people for whom American Sign Language is the only acceptable and usable mode of communication and others who are more comfortable with speech and speechreading; they also included people from a wide variety of educational, ethnic, and economic backgrounds. Naturally, the people in this diverse group differ widely in their attitudes about the hearing world, in the way they experience deafness, and in the life choices they have made.

Perhaps the most essential distinction among deaf people is whether or not they are part of the Deaf community. Not all deaf people belong to the community. A person does not become a member of the Deaf community merely by virtue of being deaf. Rather, the Deaf community is made up of people who view deafness as a fundamental part of their identity; the majority of their social interactions are with other deaf people, and they actively participate in Deaf culture. Most members of the Deaf community have attended residential schools for deaf children, and all use American Sign Language (ASL), rather than speech and speechreading, as their primary mode of communication. Other deaf people, however, see themselves as part of the larger, predominantly hearing society. Still others lie somewhere in between the deaf and hearing worlds.

A deaf individual's relationship to the Deaf community is

based on many factors. One of the most significant factors is the age at which the person became deaf. The later the onset, the more likely the person is to choose not to identify with the Deaf community. Educational background also plays a part in the decision (that is, an individual whose schooling emphasized speech and speechreading and gave little acknowledgment to ASL is likely to choose a more hearing orientation). Furthermore, people who have moderate degrees of hearing loss tend not to be members of the Deaf community. Ultimately, however, an individual's relationship with the Deaf and hearing communities depends on the effect that deafness has on that person's identity.

Unlike most societies, where cultural identity is passed from parent to child, the Deaf community is largely made up of people who have hearing parents who have had no contact with deaf people. A deaf person's membership in the Deaf community, then, is a matter of personal choice. At the root of this choice, and therefore, the deaf person's identity, lies the issue of communication. For members of the Deaf community, the essential form of communication is American Sign Language. Although ASL was long denigrated by the hearing community, especially by educators who believed deaf people should be taught to communicate orally (through speech and speechreading), ASL is now acknowledged to be a rich and highly effective form of communication. It is not, as many once thought, a method of spelling out English or of simply pantomiming what one wants to say. ASL is a language in its own right, with its own grammatical structure and a rich vocabulary that includes idioms.

Despite the acceptance of ASL as a language, educators continue to argue about which communication method is best for deaf children. This centuries-old argument has been raging in the United States and elsewhere between those who advocate the use of signing and those who advocate oralism. The controversy has become so intense at times that some oral schools have instructed the parents of deaf children to put boxing gloves on their child's hands to prevent any use of gesture. The question of speech versus sign hits at the very heart of what it means to be deaf. While oralists argue that it is only through speech that a deaf person can becoming a fully functioning member of society, advocates of sign hotly dispute that claim.

The importance of ASL to the Deaf community cannot be overemphasized. For people born deaf or deafened in early childhood, learning speech and speechreading is a tremendously difficult, time-consuming, and frustrating experience, one that is frequently unsuccessful. Even the most skilled speechreaders have difficulty understanding most speech. In contrast, ASL is a natural, expressive means of communication for deaf people. As such, ASL has become a symbol of deaf identity and the chief means by which deaf culture is transmitted from one generation to the next.

Differences in how people experience deafness are also reflected in the terms they use. While most of the writers in this anthology refer to themselves as deaf, others use the term *hard of hearing,* and a few use *hearing impaired.* This is not a minor difference, but relates in complex ways to the writer's personal experience and identity. Many—but by no means all—of the writers who describe themselves as deaf were born deaf or lost their hearing at a very young age. They are often people whose identities fall clearly within the Deaf community. On the other hand, the people who write about hearing loss or impairment tend to be people who lost their hearing as adolescents or adults. Having an orientation that is chiefly hearing, these writers present a very different view than the writers who define themselves as deaf.

The term *hard of hearing* can be somewhat confusing. For many people, hard of hearing refers to a limited or moderate degree of hearing loss; a person is hard of hearing if he or she uses hearing and speech for communication but has a mild or moderate degree of hearing impairment. However, some people with severe or profound hearing losses use the term *hard of hearing* rather than deaf to indicate that they are not members of the Deaf community and that they have a chiefly hearing identity.

The writers who have contributed to this anthology come from every perspective. They include people who were born deaf, who lost their hearing as children, or who became deaf later in life. Some of these writers use English as their medium of expression and some use American Sign Language. They define themselves as *deaf,* as *hard of hearing*, and as *hearing impaired,* and some identify with the Deaf community while others do not.

The differences in the backgrounds and personal choices made by these writers resonate throughout their works. Many, but not all, of the selections in this book specifically deal with the experience of deafness or of hearing loss. These works explore all aspects of that experience, and their emotional range sweeps from joy to despair.

Several works depict the sensory experience of deafness, and others deal with the day-to-day frustrations of hearing loss. Emily Mandelbaum's "Sounds," for example, describes the frustration of trying to make sense of the cacophonous racket that many hard of hearing people perceive. She explains that sound that once was "clear as glass" has become an "aural fog." Mandelbaum's poem depicts the mental gymnastics, second guessing, and fakery that hard of hearing people often use to keep up with the jumble of noises they remember as conversation—a barrage requiring "amplifiers, guesses, reasoning, quick solutions."

Using the wintry images of "Peter and the Wolf," Claire Blatchford's poem "The Deaf Girl" recalls the memory of music, the vivid images music evoked in the mind of a young girl, and the sense of stillness that descended with childhood deafness. These images contain fear as well as sorrow: "I . . .

could not tell where in the silence of my room, the wolves waited." But there is also a sense that the child did not simply lose her hearing, she learned a different way to hear: "I have lived with ears in my eyes."

In his angry and powerful "Practice," Raymond Luczak describes a young deaf boy trying to use the telephone. Placing the receiver against his body-worn hearing aid, he struggles to understand his father's voice at the other end of the line. As his father repeats the same phrase again and again, the boy's despair swells with every failure, until the poem ends in a burst of rage.

Along a somewhat different line, Delores Goodrick Beggs cleverly describes the sometimes agonizing physical sensation of tinnitus, the ringing or buzzing in the ears that many hard of hearing people experience. She compares her tinnitus to an incessantly ringing phone, a stuck doorbell, "sound pounding on unyielding door."

In "Christmas Cheer," Karin Mango describes the practical frustrations of hearing loss, especially those resulting from the hubbub and stress of the holidays. Confronted with visitors, Christmas carols, chatting crowds, and parties during the holiday season, Mango does what every hard of hearing person has done at some time or other—she plots her escape. Making arrangements for her family's holiday dinner, the writer plans to take a few books to a quiet spot and wait the holidays out, even though Christmas was once one of her favorite times. But Mango never goes through with her plan; instead, she chooses to get through the holidays using her wits, her sense of humor, and her lipreading skills. Mango's methods of dealing with friends and family, finding ways around the awkward socializing, and enjoying the music despite its raucous sound in her ears, provide a glimpse into the ways hard of hearing people adjust their lives and their environments to make up for lost hearing.

These works, among others, provide some sharp insights

into the practical frustrations of hearing loss and the perceptual world deaf and hard of hearing people inhabit. The majority of contributions to this anthology, however, deal with another issue: the profound impact of deafness on the individual's place in society. The overriding theme that emerges in much of this work is that the tragedy of deafness has little to do with the inability to hear and much to do with the marginal and stigmatized position of deaf people in an unaccommodating and aggressively hearing world.

Several works in this anthology lash out at the hearing community. Willy Conley's moving play *The Hearing Test* uses the complex questions surrounding cochlear implant—a surgical technique designed to improve the hearing of profoundly deaf people—to deal with issues of self-determination and choice. Michael, a boy of thirteen, is brought in for his yearly audiological examination by his well-meaning, but domineering mother. Forced to use speech and lipreading, forbidden to sign, he has been refused an identity as a deaf person. As his mother and the audiologist discuss his life, his deafness, and his future, Michael waits, frustrated but passive. However, Michael is accompanied by his alter-ego, which manifests itself as his "mind voice." Here we discover the real Michael, the person behind the quasi-hearing persona he is forced to use to cope with his mother's infantile view of him. The mind voice is articulate, mature, and competent, but unseen and unheard by his mother and the audiologist. While this real self responds with sardonic wit and righteous anger, Michael's mother and the audiologist plan a cochlear implant for him. Conley's work zeros in on two issues vital to deaf identity: society's determination to remake deaf people in the image of hearing people, and the right of a deaf person to choose a deaf identity.

In "A Wish, Unheard," Raymond Luczak also indicts the hearing community. The hearing man in his poem is the very epitome of power. As others gather around him, listening and laughing at his stories, his speech becomes a symbol and a manifestation of power itself. The deaf man, in contrast, can only observe from a distance; he is removed from the laughter, the exchange of stories, and the hearing man's power. Yet, it is the hearing man ultimately who does not hear and the deaf man's wish that remains unheard.

In "The Audiologist" Luczak writes about another aspect of the relationship between deaf and hearing people. In this case, the hearing person is an audiologist, a professional who measures hearing ability. The audiologist in Luczak's poem is hidden, concealed behind the windows of her testing booth. Headphones in place, the deaf man waits to be tested, but he hears nothing. The relationship between the deaf man and the hearing professional is one of conflict. Luczak states that "the audiologist and I are at war. . . ." But, as he makes clear, this conflict is often related to a greater struggle—"I am also at war with myself."

In her story "Inner Ears," Mary Holmes portrays a child's terror as she is given her annual hearing test. Significantly, Kate is not afraid of deafness: the child knows she cannot hear, has long been aware of the screaming tinnitus in her ears, and, for much of her young life, has managed to fake her way in a hearing world. What Kate fears is the discovery of her deafness. Even as a child, Kate is aware of what that discovery can mean to her life. She will be considered different; she will be considered less.

Other works in this anthology deal less with rage at the hearing community than with the bewilderment and confusion that often result when deaf and hearing people try to interact. In "The Finer Things," Raymond Luczak deals with issues of identity and choice. His character, a young deaf gay man who yearns to live "the good life," is forced to choose between an older, hearing man who promises to introduce him to great art, gourmet food, fine wine, and music, and his deaf-blind lover and the Deaf community.

Although many of these works reverberate with anger and frustration, others resound with joy and triumph. David Wright's feelings about his deafness, stated most cogently in his poem "Dialogue of a Deaf Man," are a case in point. The "injury" of deafness, once dominated, is an asset, Wright proclaims. Of what great importance is the human voice, after all, especially when so much of what is spoken is of so little consequence? "A twitch and a grimace" can say far more than words. More than this, Wright declares that "the human condition is the same" regardless of the circumstances of one's life, and that his deafness, being part of the divine scheme, "is a good plan."

Another of the themes dealt with by these contributors is the idea of hearing without sound. Hannah Merker's essays from *Listening*, are a testimony to the myriad ways living beings hear. Merker's dog Sheena acts as her ears; so does her husband, telling her the sound of a foghorn, of rain on melting ice. A deaf-blind friend of Merker's, on the other hand, hears with his fingertips. Animals often understand each other without the use of sound, and even plants communicate silently. Merker explores and details these and other forms of "listening."

Robert Panara's "On His Deafness," also describes hearing without ears; he hears through his sheer love of the written word. Poetry, he writes, has its own sound. The written word enables him to hear not only what is audible to hearing people—"the twinkle of a bell. . .the swish of leaves"—but much more. Poetry provides a key to a world beyond the limits of the ears, even allowing him to hear "the rustle of a star."

David Wright, in his autobiography *Deafness*, writes of unique ways of hearing. For him, "silence is not absence of sound but of movement." Wright hears a rush of noise when he sees the wind blow through the trees, a beating of wings when he sees a bird in flight. Borrowing a phrase from Wordsworth, he terms this sound without sound "eye-music."

Another recurring and consistently positive theme in this book is the love of sign language, which Panara calls "the mimic movement/of silent symphony." In "For Stanley Teaching Sign Language and Us," Anne McDonald compares sign to flying, to soaring; and in "Wing Biddlebaum," she writes of "hands talking like birds." Sign is linked to music in McDonald's poetry: "You are stirring an orchestra inside me," she writes to the man teaching her sign.

Raymond Luczak writes of being a boy in a small town, hating his voice and yearning to learn sign. Like McDonald's "For Stanley. . . ," Luczak's poem "Learning to Speak I" is an expression of his gratitude to the woman who taught him sign: "didn't you know what you had begun when you agreed to teach me my first and then the next sign until I couldn't stop. . . ?"

Edna Shipley-Conner writes of learning sign as an adult. In the first stanza of her poem "On My Impending Deafness," she links hearing loss to death: "I've been dying since my first breath." In the following two stanzas, she describes her longing to hear and asks fervently how she can live without sound and what she can do with her time, with her life. The answer to this anguished question emerges at the end of the poem: "I'll use my hands like lightning." In so doing, she transforms not only "the silence. . .into signs" but the shape of her own fear "into a new form."

For many of the writers in this book, sign is their response to the rage they feel at the hearing community. Robert Panara's "The Deaf Experience" begins with a crisp depiction of the frustrating and often unsuccessful act of speechreading; in other words, "trying to decipher/the word/unheard/the sleight of tongue." The mouth of the speaker opens and shuts to the confused and uncomprehending gaze of the speechreader. However, the second half of his poem provides a response to the pent-up frustration expressed in the first half: signing is a "reaction in action . . . A show of hands." In "Lip Service,"

Panara chastises the hearing community for its determination to use speech with deaf people and the pressure it puts on deaf people to integrate into the hearing community. If integration is so important, he advises the hearing community, then "change your line of crap from speech to sign."

The vivid rage expressed in Christopher Heuer's poem "Larynx" is also transformed in the end through sign. "Deafness has broken my nose and my teeth. . ." he begins, bitterly lamenting the place in the world assigned to those with poor speech. But Heuer's poem turns at the very end to a song in praise of signing "as I dance my way down the street/to its light vibrations."

Sign plays a different part in the works of three of the poets included in this collection. Eddie Swayze, Joseph Castronovo, and Peter Cook all compose and perform their poetry in American Sign Language. Their works are translated here, by the poets themselves, into English. Coming from a visual/gestural language, their works are strikingly different from most English poetry. To readers accustomed to the sound of poetry composed in English or other spoken languages, these poems sound unique, even strange, and their beauty is in some cases revealed visually by the spacing on the page, an analog to the performance of signed poetry.

The poets, playwrights, fiction writers, and essayists included in this anthology are writers—not simply deaf or hard of hearing writers. In addition to dealing with deafness and hearing loss, they also traverse the many facets of human experience. Trudy Drucker offers humorous verse, a sensitive treatment of imminent old age, and a tribute to Sylvia Plath. Cynthia Amerman's poetry explores birth and death using images from mythology and dreams. Willy Conley's "One Frame per Second" deals with death and memory; Lisa Fay deals with the nuclear age; and Curtis Robbins with homelessness. This collection also contains the striking nature-imagery of Claire Blatchford and Anne McDonald, Michael Winters' fantasy tale "Melusine," and Frances Parsons' unique impressions from her three-month excursion to China.

Compiling this anthology gave me the opportunity to read the work of a large number of deaf and hard of hearing people, many of whom are not professional writers. Because the purpose of this book is to present the works of writers rather than to describe the experience of deafness, I chose pieces whose primary aim was either artistic or journalistic. As a result, I had to omit many moving expressions of the deaf experience. Some of the most enjoyable poetry I read was by children. One of my favorites was the poem sent me by Stephanie Bliss and Penny Starr at the Pennsylvania School for the Deaf: "Deaf talk sign/Beautiful/. . . Happy talk sign language/with friends."

No Walls of Stone represents, I believe, the best and most representative work by contemporary deaf and hard of hearing writers. As I collected these writings, I thought about possible titles for an anthology. I searched in books about deafness and through prose and poetry of all sorts for a line that would capture the essence of the works I had selected. Ultimately, the phrase *no walls of stone* arose from my imagination. It is an attempt to distill the aim of this collection into a single line. Few groups of people have had as many walls to scale as deaf and hard of hearing people. These walls include the natural barriers that exist between worlds of sound and worlds of silence and the artificial walls erected by an uncompromising world. Even the experience of deafness has been likened to the materials from which walls are built: *stone deaf; deaf as a post.* If there is a single thread running throughout this collection, it is this: As we draw to the close of the twentieth century, human beings can no longer barricade themselves from others whose way of experiencing the world is different. We have no choice now but to break down the barriers that separate us. At this time in history, we can no longer live with walls.

Acknowledgments

Cynthia Amerman: "Game of Hide-and-Seek" and "Medusa" were published in *The Blair Review* (Summer 1990, pp. 79, 77). "Birth" was published in *The Blair Review* (Spring 1986, p. 9). "Game of Hide-and-Seek" was originally published in Spanish as "Juego al Escondite." "Woodville" was published in *Swift River* (Spring 1980, p. 17).

Claire Blatchford: "The Deaf Girl: A Memory;" "The Collector;" "Centering;" and "Acorn" were published in *Centering* (a privately published collection of poetry).

Jack Clemo: "Affirmative Way" was published in *Broad Autumn* (London: Eyre McThuen, 1975). "Whispers" was published in *A Different Drummer* (Padstow, Cornwall: Tabb House, 1986). "Helen Keller at Wrentham" and "Beethoven" were published in *The Echoing Tip* (London: Eyre McThuen, 1971).

Trudy Drucker: "Sylvia" was published in *College English Notes* (Summer 1982, p. 4). "The Fifth Voyage" was published in the *American Association of University Professors Bulletin* (Winter 1973, p. 406). "Twilight Time" was published in *The New York Times Metropolitan Diary* (September 20, 1989).

Mary Holmes: "Inner Ears" was published in *Kaleidoscope* (Summer 1990).

Raymond Luczak: "Learning to Speak I;" "Practice;" and "The Audiologist" were published in *St. Michael's Falls*. "A Wish, Unheard" was published in *Mute*. "Mrs. Kichak's Plum Tree" was published in *This Way to the Acorns* (all three volumes are privately published collections of poetry).

Karin Mango: "To Your Health" was published in *Speak Up Newsletter* (April 1985). "Christmas Cheer" was published in *The Voice* (November/December 1989, pp. 7–8).

Robert F. Panara: "Lip Service" (Spring 1983, p. 17) and "The Deaf Experience" (Spring 1976, p. 11) were published in *Gallaudet Today*. "On His Deafness" was published in *Scouting for the Deaf* (1973).

Frances M. Parsons: *I Didn't Hear the Dragon Roar* was published in 1988 (Washington, DC: Gallaudet University Press, pp. 1–2, 78, 79–80, 84, 85).

David Wright: "Dialogue of a Deaf Man" was published in *Selected Poems* (Manchester, England: Caranet, 1988). "By the Effigy of St. Cecilia" was published in *Monologue of a Deaf Man* (London: Andre Deutsch, Ltd., 1958). *Deafness* was published in 1969 (New York: Stein and Day, pp. 5–7, 8–12, 49–52).

All other works have not been previously published.

No Walls of Stone

Claire Blatchford

Born in 1944, Claire Howell Blatchford became profoundly deaf after a case of mumps at the age of six. She attended schools with hearing children and graduated from Bennington College in 1966. She has two master's degrees—one in elementary education from the Adelphi University/Waldorf School teacher training program, and one in education of the deaf from Teacher's College, Columbia University. She writes for children, teaches crafts, and lives in Guilford, Connecticut with her husband, two daughters, and a self-trained hearing ear mutt named Ginger.

The Deaf Girl: A Memory

Once as a child I heard Prokofiev
On a record given to me.
I played it all the afternoons,
Wolves followed Peter through my rooms,
Forests and snow lay about me.
And then, as if to seal the spell,
I woke one morning and could not tell
Where in the silence of my room
The wolves waited.

       The snow waited
To melt. The forest did not stir.
Peter had disappeared. Frozen
In sunlight and shadows I've lived
With ears in my eyes, eyes in my heart.
Sometimes it seems that I have heard
Peter's footsteps in my heart-beat,
Sometimes I think I've seen
The wolves passing there.

Claire Blatchford
20

The Collector

I have caught butterflies
And felt them fluttering
Between my two cupped hands.
But when my terror died
I learned to pin their wings,
To know their names and kinds.

I sought for patternings.
My mind on colored wings
Followed the hue of things
But died because my eyes
Recognized no terror
And pinned love to a name.

Claire Blatchford
21

Centering

Bring it to the center
Slowly, slowly,
Bring the clay inwards,
Push it downwards,
Urge it to the center,
Steady, steady.

Bring it to the one point
That's still, that's still
Till it seems nothing moves
Though the wheel runs round
And round.
Let the hand down:

Enter the center,
Make it like an eye, an I,
And then pull—
Pull the walls up high
Pull the soft earth
Towards the sky.

Claire Blatchford

Acorn

You will not spin for me
On your sharp pointed heel
And I would break off your cap,
Put you between my teeth and crack
Your roundness.

Yet you have a shadow,
Stillness that is palpable,
Roundness of some inevitable
Movement.

And in my anger
I find that I am holding
An oval tree.

Claire Blatchford
24

Mid-Winter

Out in the fields there
Where the grasses bend down
And the clouds roll slow
Over the sleeping earth—
I saw a single tree
Rise up and breathe out
A deep drawn "O . . ."

Robert F. Panara

Robert Panara is one of the best-known deaf writers in the United States and is well known in the American Deaf community. After becoming deaf at the age of ten, he attended public schools in New York City, including Bronx Parkway Public School #103 and De Witt Clinton High School, where he was the only deaf student. After graduating from high school, he learned about Gallaudet College (later, University), a liberal arts college for deaf students. To prepare himself for Gallaudet, Panara attended the American School for the Deaf at West Hartford, Connecticut, to learn sign language and discover his deaf identity. Upon graduating from Gallaudet, Panara became a teacher. In a career spanning forty-two years, he has taught at the New York School for the Deaf, Gallaudet University in Washington, D.C., the Rochester Institute of Technology, and the National Technical Institute for the Deaf in Rochester, New York, where he established both the English Department and the drama program. His publications include *The Silent Muse: Anthology of Poetry by the Deaf* (co-editor), *Great Deaf Americans* (co-author), and the three-volume *Gallaudet Encyclopedia of Deaf People and Deafness* (Associate Editor). Panara has been the recipient of numerous awards, including the first Teegaarden Poetry Award and the Humanitarian Award in Theatre at Gallaudet University, the Outstanding Teaching Award at Rochester Technical Institute, the Medal of Merit from the World Federation of the Deaf, and two honorary doctorates.

On His Deafness

My ears are deaf, and yet I seem to hear
Sweet nature's music and the songs of man
For I have learned from Fancy's artisan
How written words can thrill the inner ear
Just as they move the heart, and so for me
They also seem to ring out loud and free.

In silent study I have learned to tell
Each secret shade of meaning and to hear
A magic harmony, at once sincere,
That somehow notes the tinkle of a bell,
The cooing of a dove, the swish of leaves,
The raindrop's pitter-patter on the eaves,
The lover's sigh, the thrumming of guitar,
And, if I choose, the rustle of a star!

Robert F. Panara

The Deaf Experience

Looking at the speaker
thru uncomprehending
eyes
trying to decipher
the word
unheard
the sleight of tongue
and talking mouth
which opens
and shuts
instamatically
enigmatically
traumatically. . .

Reaction
in action
a flutter of fingers
a show of hands
the mimic movement
of silent symphony
suddenly
shattered
with cymbalic force
endorsed
of course
by smug recourse
to verbal intercourse.

Robert F. Panara
28

Lip Service

You want to rap
you said
and let it all hang out
this thing about
the communication gap
that keeps us separate
your kind
from mine.

You want to rap
you said
you want to integrate
but you decline
to change your line
of crap
from speech
to sign.

Anne McDonald

Anne McDonald received a B.A. from Providence College and an M.F.A. in Creative Writing from the University of Massachusetts. She has taught creative writing workshops with children at various festivals. Her work has been published in *Poetry Northwest, Milkweed Chronicle, Colorado State Review, Gumbo, Wind, Intro,* and other journals. McDonald was a co-winner of an Academy of American Poets prize while at the University of Massachusetts and won the Galway Kinnell Poetry Prize from the Pawtucket, Rhode Island Arts Council in 1984. She now works full time as a law librarian for the Rhode Island Department of Attorney General. McDonald has been profoundly deaf since the age of six.

For Stanley Teaching Sign Language and Us

"Two years blacked-out" is how you describe
losing your hearing at nine. One girl
tells: "I went to a concert signed
so beautifully I want to learn."
I don't know what to say to you. You're
stirring an orchestra inside me. I wouldn't
listen before.

Your hands fly with funny stories
about your son, the Pacific Northwest pilot.
I want to soar with you. I'm grounded
by memories. If I were an insect, these
would molt away. Your words: two years
blacked-out, no memories and "I was lucky—
I *only* lost my hearing."

I name this memory: "Nuns and the *Pater Noster*."
I was six thinking the English words
blurring my ears were Latin, afraid of nuns,
the voice of God drums through their white
bibs. These holy sisters were the first
to spot I wasn't in tune with the right voices.

They called my mother, terrified me to hell.
I got harnessed to a thing called
a hearing aid, left the Catholic school
forever. I wanted to be Joan of Arc listening
to Michael, Catherine, and Margaret. I turned
into Anne hearing shadows. My blue corduroy
jumper hates me wearing that funny bump-lump
against its chest. It tells me!

My fingers splay into signals. You will
teach them to talk and I'll fold my hands
into a sign I haven't seen yet.

Anne McDonald
31

The Deadening of October

I've counted 58 days of roadside pumpkins,
70 days since my midsummer birthday. Ridges
and warts jut from my fingers
drumming pumpkins, over the Holyoke Range. Below
the Deerfield River spawns out-of-season
salmon. I think of St. Peter, the fishing-miracle,
what would he say to Jerome, patron saint
of librarians.

November, how shall I bless your partying saints?
I'm lousy at stirring that sacred punch. See,
angelic doctors, holy martyrs hover above the church
pillars while the congregation chants
the *Confiteor* in Polish and English.

What a long glide from March 25, Angel Gabriel's
feast day, to this deadening of October!
Yet I'm full of pumpkin seeds I might wreath
into some sort of halo. Tonight
we bring in the darkness an hour early. I amass
names from *Lives of Saints*, cling to them
until they turn up as bones on All Soul's.

In six days the temperature drops to forty.
I have waited by the gilt edges
of my prayer. Wearing a bleached dress, I lift
myself into the vision's descent.
My mother glows among the hosts and hosannas,
a hunting moon. My father has me back in the fold.

Anne McDonald

Foxglove

for Don

This is implied in the animal name:
long pistiled fingers
speaking of nothing tame

but open lips; tongue plunging
down inside the flower
the way the white-tipped fox, tingling,

washes away his snakebelly-white gloves
at twilight as he fades pink before
he flowers. His burnt sienna loves

form again in little bells,
the strains from the foxflower
song of an animal crying inside his cells.

And in this pipe-thin
figwort, the ruined foxfire
distills into medicine.

Anne McDonald

Wing Biddlebaum

My hands talking like birds
give me my name, a "W" soaring
from the temple. They amaze me,
banish vowel, consonant of my baptismal
name like English sparrows. I taunt:
"roost-pigeon," "piss-smell."

In answer: the handshape: "dream."
The "need" finger drifts,
shows me bright animals, prey
of air. I learn to link
the scarlet tanager
with scarlet fever. I'm
the shamed red woman, waiting
for cities to rise after
Babel, from a language of shapes.

In this night-anchor, my hand-
birds claim a field-harvest:
church, tree, fireflies.

Anne McDonald
35

Speaking About the Deaf Child

My play's a voice in a puppet
theater with only my tongue
for an audience. I unfurl
ballet words, translate
the wind's tongue
Into conch shell language.

People imagine I'm velvet
flung into a tree-nest
while I prance outside their gates.
But gratings from their inner
worlds reach me through my toes.

And I dance myself out
of my dance in tune to drums
you beat around me, teaching
a new subject you call "advanced
vibrations." Silent flamingo-
hairdressers: missionaries,
touch me.

Anne McDonald

Willy Conley

Willy Conley, a former actor with the National Theatre of the Deaf, graduated with an M.A. in Creative Writing from Boston University. His plays have won the American Deaf Drama Award, the Sam Edwards Deaf Playwrights Competition and, recently, an award and production from the Baltimore Playwrights Festival for *The Hearing Test*. The play was also produced at the Boston Playwrights Theatre. One of his other plays, *Broken Spokes,* was produced off-off Broadway and at the University of Texas at Dallas. Some of his writings have appeared in *Kaleidoscope, Uncharted, Inbetween,* and *NTID focus*. Conley holds a B.S. degree in Biomedical Photographic Communication from the Rochester Institute of Technology, and he is certified as a Registered Biological Photographer. Conley teaches in the English department at Gallaudet University.

One Frame per Second

he died

It's hard to watch my mother go
through clips of her life: grey
polaroids of childhood, tattered
prints of her parents, her father's
army medals, her mother's jewelry.

alone on a winter night

She touches each relic and stares
a memory slides in superimposed.
She grows still and watches each
part of her past.

in his bedroom —

The object is laid back on the table
and another is held. One memory
segues to the next: her ritual of grief.
One day it will be me touching her
belongings.

shot himself, my grandfather

The Seawall

Towards the east end of Galveston Island, where the seawall rises higher, motels and convenience stores buzz with flourescent lights and green and red neons. Cars quickly pull in and out, never staying for more than five minutes. Closer to the end of the island stands the University of Texas Medical Branch. On the fourth floor, in O.R. #2, preparation for emergency surgery was underway for a burn victim brought in from an offshore oil explosion. A medical photographer waited to photograph the patient's burns for insurance purposes. The photographer leaned against the wall while nurses cut away the patient's clothes. The doctors stood around a draped table readied with surgical tools. One whispered something into the ear of the other, their laughter hidden from the photographer by their face masks. The photographer yawned and looked at his watch.

A nurse came over to the photographer and wrote something in pen on her scrub pants. The photographer read the message on her thigh and nodded, gesturing okay with his fingers. He looked at the burn patient and then went out the door, leaving his camera equipment on a small table.

Outside the sterile core of operating rooms, a man waited by the switchboard window where a receptionist handled operation schedules and emergency calls. The photographer stopped halfway down the hall when he saw who was by the window. He shook his head and then proceeded. The man gave him a big smile and waved hello.

"You're not supposed to see me in this area, Gustavo," said the photographer.

"You told me okay visit you hospital here," Gustavo replied.

"No, only in the photo lab—in the basement, I said. Remember? How did you find me here?"

"Other photographer told me. Me finish visit basement, you not there. He told me you here. Me need talk with you."

"I'm not supposed to be talking here. I could get fired. Now you go. We'll talk later."

"Meet lab later?"

"No, I prefer outside of the hospital. We talk too much at the lab. It's not good," the man said.

"Why?" asked Gustavo.

"Makes me look like I'm socializing all the time at work. Please, I'll meet you later. Just tell me where, I'll show up, okay?"

"Meet restaurant, near wall. Know where?"

"The seawall's ninety blocks long. How am I supposed to know?" asked the man.

"You know, red, blue lights, pretty. H . . . something."

"Yeah, yeah, I know. Go on. See you later. My beeper is vibrating; I gotta get back," the man said.

The street light glare along the seawall boulevard gave the breaking surf a bile color. Offshore, oil rigs outlined by beacons continued to suck into the night. Cars and people drifted by slowly through the humidity. The only bright spot was the blinking neon sign, HOLLYWOOD CAFE, that hung behind the salt-misted window. Behind the window, the man stared across the red formica table at Gustavo.

"Why did you steal it?," the man asked. He was chewing on his moustache.

"My son," said Gustavo.

"But your son is too young to want one. Besides, he probably won't have any use for it when he gets older."

"I want sell, get money."

"What do you need the money for? Gustavo, look at me."

Gustavo rolled the salt shaker between his palms, a Gerber baby food jar with fork holes poked through the lid. The baby's smiling face on the label was almost gone.

"I want buy son hot dog," said Gustavo.

"A hot dog?"

"On seawall, Saturday."

"I could've given you money for that, Gus. You know I would. I gave you my good pants didn't I?"

A waitress with crossed eyes came over to take their order. The man couldn't tell if she was looking at him or Gustavo. He went ahead and wrote on his napkin, asking for their list of Mexican beers. She shook her head and pointed to a Budweiser sign.

"They only have Bud here?" the man asked Gustavo.

"Here cheap," said Gustavo.

The man gave the waitress an "okay" gesture.

"I can't believe it, no Tecate?" the man asked. This is a Mexican joint, am I right?"

"Yeah."

"You come here a lot?"

"Fridays. Free coffee."

The waitress returned with two cans of beer with pieces of ice floating on the rims. The man looked around at the customers. A couple of men at the counter near the window stared listlessly into the holes of their beer cans. A fat couple at the other end were petting and necking. In the corner booth, a dark, emaciated old man coughed hard. Bits of food shot out of his mouth.

"Your pants. Broken," said Gustavo. He toyed with a piece of ice with his tongue.

"You broke my pants?"

"Zipper."

"Aw, I don't care. Gustavo . . . Gustavo, look at me."

"You disappointed . . . me?" he asked.

"Well no . . . yeah, yes. Look at me. That doesn't mean I'm going to stop being your friend. What's your sign down in Mexico for friend? I forget."

"Amigo," he said.

"Yeah, that's it. Amigo. You and me, amigos. But, if you get caught I won't have the bucks to bail you out."

The man slapped at a mosquito and flicked it off of his arm.

"You photographer," said Gustavo.

"That doesn't make me rich. And it doesn't mean you can feel free to steal tape decks or whatever from K-Mart 'cause your amigo can save you everytime."

"You take beautiful skilled pictures."

"So?"

"Many dollars in your pocket."

No way, I'm barely getting by. Nobody's buying my work, and you know what? Gus . . . I hate it when you look away. What're you looking at?"

"Poor man there."

The dark man in the corner picked up a plastic wrapper off the floor and used it to cover his hand to eat his roll. He slid on three pats of butter, took a bite, and washed it down with a swig from his brown quart bottle. Beer dribbled down his chin. He coughed again, spraying bits of bread. When he finished his roll he crumpled up the wrapper and threw it back on the floor. He hawked a wad of phlegm and spat it under the table.

"I'm still paying off my camera equipment, my bicycle, TV and, on top of that, rent and food."

"You rich."

"Come off it, I'm not rich. Now, where's the tape deck—in your car?"

"Yeah. In sleep bag."

"Are you sleeping in your car again?" Don't tell me. . .you can't pay for your room anymore."

Gustavo picked out dirt from under his fingernails with a fork.

"Look . . . your wife's family can't do this to you," said the man.

"See son two hours, Saturdays now."

"They cut down your visiting hours?"

"Told me court order."

"They're liars!"

"I good father . . . bring flowers for wife, tell her I love her. She not understand—mental retard, you know. Her mother, sister protect her. They ask me, 'Where money? Where money?'"

"Do you give them all your money?"

"Mother take . . . for boy."

"Do you give them all your money every Saturday?"

"Yeah."

"You work your ass off every night cleaning the cinema and then give your whole paycheck to that woman?"

"I want see my boy."

"Hide some of it. They won't know."

"They know. I don't care money. Son want see me bad. I deaf, he deaf—we same. I make son laugh."

Gustavo rolled the pepper shaker, which still had its label intact. He stared at the baby's picture. The man looked at the black velvet pictures of valiant toreadors hanging crooked on the wall.

"Gustavo . . . I'm leaving here for good next week. I've got to get off this island."

"What wrong? Don't like here?"

"Nothing. I like Galveston. I like drinking beers with you in the cinema. . ."

"Where you go?"

"California."

"California have Tecate, lime, salt?"

"Yes."

"Can I go with?"

"I can't"

"Why? You, me, amigo. Live together, eat together, lie in sun together."

"NO! I'm sorry. I must go . . . alone."

The man paid for the beers and handed Gustavo a $50 bill. He gave Gustavo a quick hug and then hurried out the door. He stopped to look both ways before he crossed the boulevard to get to the seawall. Fifteen feet below the man watched the murky water swish garbage around the boulders. He started to walk west but stopped and looked back. Gustavo was still sitting at the table with his back to the gulf.

The Hearing Test
(A one-act play)

Characters:

MICHAEL—deaf with barely intelligible speech; wears a hearing aid outside of his shirt—a large body aid with straps.

MICHAEL'S MIND VOICE—deaf and doesn't speak; fluent in use of American Sign Language; looks older and masculine.

MRS. GOLDMAN—Michael's mother

DR. SNYDER—Michael's audiologist

RADIO ANNOUNCER—confined to the radio booth, he has the dual role of radio announcer and being the speaking voice of Michael's Mind Voice.

Time: 1988

Setting: An audiological testing area. There are four distinct areas to this space: the old waiting room, the audiologist's testing booth where standard hearing tests are given, the sound booth where the patient sits, and the radio announcer's booth. Since the radio booth is not realistically a part of an audiological set-up, it should be placed somewhere upstage on a higher plane than the other areas. A table with an antique lamp and a 1940s-style radio should be included in the waiting room.

Willy Conley

Note: Sign language interpreters for Mrs. Goldman, Dr. Snyder, and the radio announcer should be on stage, somewhere off center stage but in a place where deaf audience members can easily follow the dialogue. Michael's lines should *not* be interpreted because he is not to be understood by the audience. Michael's Mind Voice should have free rein over the set, but Michael's movements are restricted; Michael's Mind Voice cannot be seen by Mrs. Goldman or Dr. Snyder.

> *Radio music plays as the audience enters the house. Occasionally, the changing of the stations should be heard. At curtain, when the house goes black, the final station should be changed to WEZY with easy-listening music. The orange glow of tubes comes up from the exposed back of the radio. An ON AIR light flicks on from the radio booth. Light up on the radio booth.*

RADIO ANNOUNCER: W-E-Z-Y, Baltimore! This is Johnny Ride. If you've just tuned in to 88.9 AM, you're in for a real treat this afternoon. For your easy-listening pleasure, we've got a line-up of famous Georges: . . .

> *A light comes up slowly on Michael at the waiting room table with the antique lamp and radio. Bored, he carves into the table with his Swiss Army knife. Michael's Mind Voice, in dark mechanic's coveralls, watches. Michael puts the knife away and tries to turn on the lamp. He notices that the wiring is still frayed at the plug.*

. . . George Winston, George Benson, Gheorghe Zamfir, and, our local legend, George and the Mella Fellas. And now to bring us the lustrous colors of autumn over the airwaves—George Winston.

MICHAEL'S MIND VOICE: . . . can't shut it out . . . still remember they called it that creepy name—a Galvanic Skin Response

Test . . . these electrodes stuck to my arms, legs, my face . . . all hooked up to an EKG or EEG—something like that . . . then they put the earphones on, like a vise . . . suddenly these electric tingles come from the wires . . . little scraggly blue lines showed up on the readout.

Light slowly comes up revealing the old waiting room with Mrs. Goldman sitting.

MRS. GOLDMAN: Michael.

Michael puts the wire down and picks up a copy of **People Magazine.**

MICHAEL'S MIND VOICE: . . . they were checking out my nervous system . . .

MRS. GOLDMAN: Hey Mike.

MICHAEL'S MIND VOICE: . . . I didn't know what a hearing test was for.

MRS. GOLDMAN: Mi-chael! Mi—oh, now you look. Do you have fresh batteries in your hearing aids?

MICHAEL: Yeah, Ma. Got Duracell batteries in there!

MRS. GOLDMAN: Okay, okay. I was just checking. It didn't seem like they were working.

MICHAEL: Buh-buh-buh . . . yeah, they work.

MRS. GOLDMAN: Please don't slap your hearing aids like that.

MICHAEL: 'Kay.

MICHAEL'S MIND VOICE: *(Slapping his chest repeatedly)* I can slap it all I want. It's mine, right? *(pause)*

Michael comforts himself with low, funny-sounding hums.

I can still feel the pain of that white tape being stripped off my skin . . . if I tell some friends about it they'll think, "so,

what's the big deal?" But God, I was three years old—
MRS. GOLDMAN: Shhh.

Michael stops humming.

MICHAEL'S MIND VOICE: Had hair on my arms and legs—
blonde . . . when that tape ripped off, little blonde hair
stuck on the tape . . . I thought that my hair would never
grow back and that made me cry more than the sting itself
. . . it's the earliest thing I can remember of something
being taken away that belonged to me.

(silence)

MICHAEL: *(excitedly)* Ma! Marlee Matlin in *People Magazine.*
Look!
MRS. GOLDMAN: Michael, honey, I'm right here—you don't have
to talk so loud. Wait a minute. Your hearing aid's whistling.

Michael fiddles with his hearing aid.

Okay, it stopped now. What is it you want me to look at,
hon? *People Magazine.* Peo-ple Ma-ga-zine.
MICHAEL: Aw, Ma.
MRS. GOLDMAN: Don't disappoint me. Say it.
MICHAEL: 'Kay. People Magazine.
MRS. GOLDMAN: You're still shouting, hon. Lower your voice.
MICHAEL: People Magazine.
MRS. GOLDMAN: Good, that's better. We still need to do a little
work on your consonants.
MICHAEL: 'Kay.
RADIO ANNOUNCER: That was George Winston's "Autumn."

Michael points to a photograph in the magazine.

RADIO ANNOUNCER: You're listening to W-E-Z-Y 88.9.

MRS. GOLDMAN: Shhh!

RADIO ANNOUNCER: I'm Johnny Ride and it is 3:30 p.m. in Baltimore's Best . . .

MRS. GOLDMAN: I'm listening for a traffic report.

RADIO ANNOUNCER: . . . and now for a quick weather and sports report. It is still sunny out with the temperature stabilizing around 63 degrees . . . the Baltimore Orioles lead the Red Sox 3-2 at the top of the 8th inning . . . rush hour traffic is picking up and . . .

MICHAEL: Ma, look—Marlee Matlin.

MRS. GOLDMAN: Shhh. I'm still listening, hon.

Michael's Mind Voice goes to the radio and feels it.

RADIO ANNOUNCER: . . . our Eye-in-the-Sky indicates we're getting a back-up on the beltway over by Jones Falls Expressway. Traffic is bottlenecked to one lane. A car had a tire blowout and can't seem to get over onto the right shoulder. Motorists entering Jones Falls are advised to take Route 50. And that's our report for the half-hour. Now for some George Benson.

MICHAEL: What did radio say?

MRS. GOLDMAN: Not saying much.

MICHAEL: Ma, tell me.

MRS. GOLDMAN: It's nothing you need to know, honey.

MICHAEL: *(pause)* Ma.

MRS. GOLDMAN: What, hon?

MICHAEL: Look.

MRS. GOLDMAN: What? . . . who's she, a model? . . . Marlee Matlin. Academy award winner for best actress . . . *Children of a Lesser God . . . (reads further)* . . . yes, I remember the movie, and . . . ?

MICHAEL: She's deaf. That wild? I never seen deaf in magazine before.

MRS. GOLDMAN: A deaf person in a magazine. Well, I suppose this is a first, but that magazine is trash. This tells people sign language is wonderful. You know I strongly disagree with that.

MICHAEL: But Marlee Matlin talk!

MRS. GOLDMAN: Yes, Marlee talks, I read that. But, she didn't use her speech skills in that movie. And all of those other deaf people flailing their hands in that awful way—bastardizing the English language. You understand what I'm saying?

MICHAEL: Uh, well yeah, but she has good—

MRS. GOLDMAN: What are hearing people out there in the world going to think when they see that? Hmmm? Someday—

MICHAEL: But, she did have good English—

MRS. GOLDMAN: Don't interrupt while I'm talking, hon.

MICHAEL: Sorry.

MRS. GOLDMAN: Someday, when you go out into that hearing world looking for a job, nobody, I'm telling you right now, nobody is going to give you a job if you flutter your hands around like those deaf people peddling ABC cards. That bothers me. All of those Hollywood producers exploiting sign language when they should be glorifying good speech coming out of deaf people. Come here, let me fix your tie. You're a good-looking boy, know that?

MICHAEL: *(pause)* What about Davey Frischberg?

MRS. GOLDMAN: What about him, hon?

MICHAEL: What did his mother talk about?

MRS. GOLDMAN: You didn't catch what his mother said?

MICHAEL: No.

MRS. GOLDMAN: Davey is learning to play the piano.

MICHAEL: Pee-ow?

MRS. GOLDMAN: Pi-a-no.

MICHAEL: Pee-now?

MRS. GOLDMAN: Not bad.

MICHAEL: He learned to play, how? He deaf like me.

MRS. GOLDMAN: He reads music uh . . . like how you read the owner's manual for the truck. Now, if your father and I bought a piano, would you like to learn how to play? Wouldn't that be wonderful? Hmmm?

MICHAEL: I need new tires for my truck.

MRS. GOLDMAN: Uh-uh, we're not spending any more money on that old truck.

MICHAEL: Aw Ma, I want—

MRS. GOLDMAN: You're whistling again. Dr. Snyder's probably going to say you'll need new earmolds. Here, let me see them.

MICHAEL: They're fine.

MRS. GOLDMAN: Honey, come on. Take them out.

MICHAEL: *(walking away)* Nah.

MRS. GOLDMAN: Please, hon?

MICHAEL: Nah!

Mrs. Goldman comes up from behind and plucks out his earmolds.

MRS. GOLDMAN: Ughhh! They're filthy, Michael!

MICHAEL'S MIND VOICE: It's not filth, it's ear wax.

MRS. GOLDMAN: *(pulling Michael back to the couch with his hearing aid cords as if they were a leash)* I thought we agreed that I would stop reminding you to clean them. Hmmmm?

MICHAEL: Yeah. MICHAEL'S MIND VOICE: Yeah.

MRS. GOLDMAN: You told me you were a big boy and that you would keep those clean every week by yourself.

MICHAEL: Yeah.   MICHAEL'S MIND VOICE: Yeah.

MRS. GOLDMAN: What's Dr. Snyder going to think when she sees them?

MICHAEL'S MIND VOICE: She's gonna shit in her underwear.

MICHAEL: Um . . .

MRS. GOLDMAN: Huh? What are you smiling about? *(pause)*

She's going to think we're a bunch of scuz.

MICHAEL: What?

MRS. GOLDMAN: Scuz. *(writes the letters with her finger on the palm of her hand)* S-C-U-Z—dirty. I trusted you to keep them clean.

MICHAEL'S MIND VOICE: *(pulls out a can of Gumout from his back pocket)* With what? Gumout?

MICHAEL: Forgot.

MICHAEL'S MIND VOICE: I was helping Dad clean out the carburetor. Can't remember to clean out earmolds, I've got no use for them.

MRS. GOLDMAN: *(wipes wax off the earmolds)* I hope Dr. Snyder doesn't notice your forgetfulness. She has a lot of influence, you know.

MICHAEL: Fluids?

MRS. GOLDMAN: In-fluence. Influence. She's the vice president of the Alexander Graham Bell Association, she's on the board of Clarke School for the Deaf . . . lots of influence.

MICHAEL'S MIND VOICE: Oh . . . all oral organizations.

MRS. GOLDMAN: Never know, she might help us out someday.

MICHAEL: How?

MRS. GOLDMAN: Maybe get you into a good college. Maybe ask you to be a role model for other deaf children to learn to speak like you. Remember, try not to gesture too much around her. You know how she's a stickler for speech and lipreading. I don't want her thinking that we don't try hard enough to raise you right as a full-functioning deaf person.

Dr. Snyder, in the business for 30 years, enters. Ironically, she is not easy to lipread. Michael's Mind Voice gets on his knees and bows to her like praising Allah.

DR. SNYDER: Aha! No need to worry about that, Mrs. Goldman. I know that you and your husband devote a lot of time and money toward Michael's well-being.

MICHAEL'S MIND VOICE: My God, she's getting bald.

DR. SNYDER: Good to see you, Michael. How've you been?

MICHAEL: F-fine.

DR. SNYDER: And how are things at Ridgely Jr. High?

MICHAEL: Whah?

DR. SNYDER: How - are - things - at - school?

MICHAEL: 'Kay.

MICHAEL'S MIND VOICE: *(in falsetto)* Oh, it's swell. We get to fin-gerpaint, we have milk and cookies and we get to go to the zoo and see—

MRS. GOLDMAN: Say—tell her about your science project.

MICHAEL'S MIND VOICE: Aw Ma, that was a long time ago!

MICHAEL: Well . . .

MRS. GOLDMAN: Go ahead.

MICHAEL'S MIND VOICE: Well, here we go again.

Reluctantly, Michael's Mind Voice signs what Michael says.

MICHAEL: I made an electric board with five science questions on the left side and five answers on right side and—sorry. Five answers on right side. And the answers are all mixed up on the right side.

DR. SNYDER: *(under her breath)* I'm sorry, what is he saying, Mrs. Goldman?

MRS. GOLDMAN: He made an electric board with five science questions—don't use your hands, Michael—and the answers are all scrambled on the right side.

DR. SNYDER: That's wonderful! It sounds so complicated!

MICHAEL'S MIND VOICE: I'm sorry your life is so simple.

MRS. GOLDMAN: Go on. Tell her about the buzzer.

MICHAEL'S MIND VOICE: Grrrrr. . . .

Michael and Mrs. Goldman speak at the same time, Mrs. Goldman repeats what Michael says.

MICHAEL: When someone pick question he have to take wire and touch the screw like this . . . *(demonstrates)* sorry . . . and they look for correct answer on the right side. Right . . . and when he find answer, he gets the wire and touch the screw. If it's right, the board will go AAAAAAAAAAHHHHH!

MRS. GOLDMAN: When someone picks a question, he takes the wire connected to the question and—sit on your hands, honey—and they look for the correct answer on the right side. Right? When the person thinks he's found the answer, he takes the wire and touches the screw next to the answer. If it's the correct answer, the electric board will—*(embarrassed)* Yes, it sort of buzzes like that.

MICHAEL: Yeah.

DR. SNYDER: Fantastic. Mrs. Goldman, isn't it wonderful to have brains? Michael, I told you, you were a smart young man. And I must tell you something—

MICHAEL: Whahshestay?

MRS. GOLDMAN: *(in undertones)* Shhh, pay attention.

DR. SNYDER: I find your speech gets better and better each year you come to see me. And you are now what . . . *(checks his file and lets out a whistle of fake surprise)* thirteen! Imagine, thirteen already. By the time you're a senior in high school you will be speaking normally like everyone else.

MRS. GOLDMAN: *(undertones)* Thirteen! Good speech.

MICHAEL'S MIND VOICE: ARF! ARF! Do I get a milk bone?

MRS. GOLDMAN: *(in a normal tone)* See, what did I tell you?

DR. SNYDER: Michael, have you been looking up the pronunciation and definition of five words in the dictionary everyday like I suggested?

MRS. GOLDMAN: *(undertones)* You look in the dictionary for—

DR. SNYDER: Let him look at me.

MICHAEL'S MIND VOICE: Arf? Oh man, the dictionary bit—

DR. SNYDER: *(louder and with some gestures)* Have you been looking up words in the dictionary?

MICHAEL'S MIND VOICE: Just say yes.

MICHAEL: Yeh-ma'am.

DR. SNYDER: Michael, have your hearing aids been working okay?

MICHAEL: Huh?

Michael's Mind Voice laughs silently.

DR. SNYDER: Your hearing—

MRS. GOLDMAN: *(undertones)* Your hearing aids—oops, sorry Dr. Snyder.

MICHAEL'S MIND VOICE: *(laughing)* Snyder, you still fall for that one.

DR. SNYDER: Please let Michael try to communicate with me, okay?

MRS. GOLDMAN: Yes ma'am.

DR. SNYDER: Let me see the volume level you have them set on. Come here. Michael—yoo-hoo. Come here . . . hmmm . . . these numbers are starting to fade.

DR. SNYDER: Is that set on 3? For your left ear? And this 3 and a half for the right?

MICHAEL: Whuh?

MRS. GOLDMAN: Yes, that's a 3. Honey, she wants to know . . .

DR. SNYDER: Mrs. Goldman, please!

MRS. GOLDMAN: Oh, I'm sorry. I'm sorry.

MICHAEL: Ma, don't call me honey, please.

MRS. GOLDMAN: I'm sorry. I won't call you honey.

DR. SNYDER: He should be able to have them set for at least level 5 to get the most out of his aids. Take your earmolds out for me, please.

MICHAEL: Whuh?

DR. SNYDER: Take - your - earmolds - out.

Mrs. Goldman gestures behind Dr. Snyder for Michael to pull out his earmolds. Michael plucks out his earmolds.

DR. SNYDER: Turn your hearing aid off! Turn it off, turn it off! That feedback. Ugh! Pierces right in my eardrums . . . here, let me see . . . oh my. When was the last time you cleaned these?

MICHAEL: Um . . . three months ago.

MICHAEL'S MIND VOICE: Wanna borrow some Gumout?

DR. SNYDER: *(pause; to Mrs. Goldman)* I understood him. Michael, why won't you clean these once a week?

MICHAEL: I want the small kind, like President Reagan.

DR. SNYDER: No. What President Reagan wears is not very strong. He has a very mild hearing loss. Your body aid is the most powerful aid on the market today. Now which is more important—your appearance or ability to hear? *(no reply)* You go ahead and seat yourself in the sound room. I'll be right with you.

RADIO ANNOUNCER: Well folks, if you're still with us, you'll know that was from the king of suave.

Michael exits. Michael's Mind Voice follows him out but stops, comes back to watch the women talk about him.

DR. SNYDER: Mrs. Goldman, there's a new hearing device that would be better for Michael. It has just passed the experimental phase and I want to discuss its possibilities after the test.

Mrs. Goldman and Dr. Snyder exit. Michael's Mind Voice crosses to the sound booth while Michael enters the same room. The light for this room should be harsh. The women enter the testing booth. Dr. Snyder checks Michael's ears with an otoscope. She dips a cotton swab in baby oil and proceeds to clean both ears.

RADIO ANNOUNCER: W-E-Z-Y. Baltimore! *(station identification tune plays)* This is Johnny Ride and it's 3:50 p.m. Coming up, we've got some extraordinary tunes for you from the king of the pan flute. But first a message from Carpet Country . . . it's the deal of the decade, that's right, Run! Fly! but don't walk down to Carpet Country. Why? There's a sale. Yes! A colossal sale with miles and miles of carpets, rugs, mats, and tapestries. We've got all kinds of fantastic designs, fabulous colors at phenomenal prices. So, come on down to 3505 Belair Road and look out for flying carpets . . . and now, the man who has reinvented the pan flute, Gheorghe Zamfir.

MICHAEL'S MIND VOICE: Ooooh! Nothing feels as good as an oily Q-tip sliding in and out of the ear. Only thing to look forward to during all this bullshit . . . year in, year out . . . check out these dead ears . . . Ma, you've got to realize these ears aren't getting any better, and they ain't getting any deader either.

DR. SNYDER: All of this wax here can really throw off the accuracy of a hearing test.

MICHAEL'S MIND VOICE: You oughta save your money. Buy yourself and Dad a subscription to the opera or take that trip to Europe you always talk about but say is too expensive . . . no wonder you can't afford it—you waste all of your money on these tests . . . *(groans)* ooohh, god damn that's good . . . Ma, I swear you look up to Dr. Snyder like some God.

DR. SNYDER: By the way, you are going to have to have some new molds made—these have shrunk a bit, which explains all of the unnecessary feedback. And besides, they're filthy.

MRS. GOLDMAN: Yes ma'am. I'll take him to have new molds made.

DR. SNYDER: Okay. You're all cleaned out. We're going to test both ears now with earphones.

Dr. Snyder puts earphones on him. She and Mrs. Goldman leave for the testing booth. Michael adjusts his chair so that he faces the window.

MICHAEL'S MIND VOICE: Hmmm. I always wonder why this little room is so full of tiny holes in the wall and ceiling. I bet if some kid doesn't try hard enough to speak well, Snyder lets poisonous gas come through those holes . . . the kid would suffocate while trying to kick open that big icebox door.

> *Lights go on in the adjacent testing booth. Dr. Snyder clicks on her microphone.*

DR. SNYDER: Okay Michael, I'm almost ready. Can you hear me all right?

> *Michael makes a gesture of "a little bit" with his fingers.*

MICHAEL'S MIND VOICE: I don't hear you, you know . . . I just feel vibrations from this vise you put on my head.
DR. SNYDER: Is that better?

> *Michael gestures "okay."*

MICHAEL'S MIND VOICE: Whatever makes you happy, you rich, old b . . .
DR. SNYDER: We're going to test your pure tone average first. Raise your right hand anytime you think . . .

> *She continues mouthing the rest of the sentence silently as Michael's Mind Voice blocks it out.*

. . . you hear the beep. I will begin with your right ear, and then your left.
MICHAEL'S MIND VOICE: Yeah, yeah . . . I know, the old raise-the right-hand-anytime-you-hear-the-beep trick . . . what do you take me for? . . . been coming here for eleven years,

get the same test, the same chair, earphones, and even the same tiny holes in the ceiling . . . well, there's a ceiling stain in the corner I didn't notice last year . . . must be recent . . .

A loud beep goes off. Michael raises his hand. Each subsequent beep gets softer and Michael "hears" only a few more and then doesn't respond to the rest that follow.

Lights go dim. The actors freeze. There's a quick flash of strong light. The lights come back up and the actors change position in preparation for the bone conduction test. Michael takes off his earphones and puts on a special headphone for the bone conduction test.

Dr. Snyder: Okay, we're all set for the bone conduction test. Ready?

Michael's Mind Voice: Chinese water torture . . . come on, hurry—get this over with.

The bone conduction test begins with a loud buzz. Each subsequent buzz becomes softer. Michael gives the usual conditioned response of raising his right hand. Lights dim. Actors freeze. There's another flash of light. Then, the lights come back up.

Mrs. Goldman comes around to Michael's side as he takes off his special headphone. Dr. Snyder stays behind working on the audiogram.

Mrs. Goldman: How are you doing?

Michael: *(Rubs the soreness on his head from the headphones)* Fine.

Mrs. Goldman: When we get done, we'll get some ice cream around the corner. How's that sound?

MICHAEL: Aw Ma. I want work on my truck now.

MRS. GOLDMAN: You'll get back to your truck soon. This won't take long. Is your head okay?

Mrs. Goldman physically comforts Michael.

MICHAEL'S MIND VOICE: No! Stop babying me—you've taken me to that ice cream place every year . . . Got cavities to prove it. *(pause)* No. Can't . . . you're too good to me, help with homework, vocabulary . . . stick up for me when you catch the guys making fun of me . . . remind me I'm not stupid . . . sometimes I think you're lying.

DR. SNYDER: Mrs. Goldman, time for spondee words. Have Michael put his hearing aids back on.

MRS. GOLDMAN: Put your hearing aids back in. See you later.

MICHAEL'S MIND VOICE: You're the best friend I've got . . . I mean Dad's my buddy 'cause of sports and all, but you're close . . . I wouldn't be who I am now if it wasn't for you . . . but why don't you want me to learn sign language?

DR. SNYDER: Okay, Michael. Try your best to hear the words I say and repeat them back to me. Okay? Good. Here we go: *(covers her mouth with a big white card)* Hot dog.

MICHAEL'S MIND VOICE: *(signs "football")*

MICHAEL: Um . . . football?

DR. SNYDER: Eye brow.

MICHAEL'S MIND VOICE: *(signs "hot dog")*

MICHAEL: Hot dog.

DR. SNYDER: Airplane.

MICHAEL'S MIND VOICE: *(signs "hair spray")*

MICHAEL: Hair spray.

DR. SNYDER: Baseball.

MICHAEL'S MIND VOICE: *(gestures "8 ball," as in playing pool)*

MICHAEL: Eight ball.

DR. SNYDER: Toothbrush.

MICHAEL'S MIND VOICE: *(signs "huge truck")*

MICHAEL: Huge truck.

DR. SNYDER: Wash cloth.

MICHAEL'S MIND VOICE: *(signs "why-not")*

MICHAEL: Why not.

DR. SNYDER: Duck soup.

MICHAEL'S MIND VOICE: *(perplexed; stops signing; shakes his head)*

MICHAEL: Ummm . . .

MICHAEL'S MIND VOICE: *(universal gesture for "fuck you")*

DR. SNYDER: That's all. Very good, Michael. *(she gestures for him to take his hearing aids off)*

MICHAEL'S MIND VOICE: Oh no, here it comes. Time for a nap.

> *Michael turns his chair around with his back to Dr. Snyder. He pulls out his earmolds. Michael's Mind Voice goes to sleep lying on the floor near Michael or sitting up against one of the speakers. Dr. Snyder comes around with the following: a baby rattle, a whistle, and a bike horn. She creates sounds next to Michael's ear. Michael stares ahead showing no reaction.*

DR. SNYDER: Hear anything?

> *Michael shakes his head. Dr. Snyder goes back to the testing booth.*

DR. SNYDER: *(to Mrs. Goldman)* Now we'll test his loudness threshold.

MRS. GOLDMAN: Please go easy on him.

DR. SNYDER: I keep reassuring you it will never happen. I know the threshold before an eardrum can burst. Never have I gone beyond that point.

> *Dr Snyder plays a recorded sentence, over and over, increasing the loudness each time.*

Let's not be late for lunch.

(Twice as loud) Let's not be late for lunch.

(louder) Let's not be late for lunch.

(louder) Let's not be late for lunch.

(louder) Let's not be late for lunch.

> *The sound increases to the loudest tolerable level for the audience. Michael's Mind Voice slowly awakens. He feels the speaker.*

(same level) Let's not be late for lunch.

(same level) Let's not be late for lunch.

DR. SNYDER: That's it. Still doesn't affect him one bit.

RADIO ANNOUNCER: I'll tell ya, Zamfir, the king of the pan flute still reigns.

> *The women exit. Michael slowly gets up and exits, feeling the speaker on his way out. Michael's Mind Voice stays behind and sits on the chair.*

RADIO ANNOUNCER: For those of you up on wind instruments that was "Siciliana" from the Concerto in F. And, I've got one more for you from the famous flautist, "Jesu Joy of Man's Desiring."

MICHAEL'S MIND VOICE: Can't figure out what that sentence says . . . bahm-bahm, bahm-bahm, bahm-bahm . . . always feels like some big steam train getting started up.

> *Lights come up on the waiting area. Dr. Snyder and Mrs. Goldman are mouthing words in silence. Actors may need to ad-lib words in silence where it feels necessary.*

> *Michael's Mind Voice crosses from the testing area to the waiting area.*

Willy Conley

MICHAEL'S MIND VOICE: Ma why won't you tell me what that sentence says . . . "no, it's confidential."

MRS. GOLDMAN: *(softly)* So how many children have had this operation?

DR. SNYDER: *(softly)* About 150. And half of them were under the age of five.

MRS. GOLDMAN: *(softly)* That many already? *(with full voice)* Will this uh thing help?

DR. SNYDER: It's called a cochlear ear implant.

MRS. GOLDMAN: Thank you. So this cochlear thing . . . will it help Michael's speech?

DR. SNYDER: Absolutely. Actually a patient's lipreading skills improve.

Michael enters putting on his hearing aids.

MRS. GOLDMAN: Fantastic!

DR. SNYDER: Also, because of the surgical nature of this experiment with the inner ear, all candidates—Michael, your hearing aid is whistling.

Michael makes the whistling stop

DR. SNYDER: That's better. Go have a seat. I'll be right with you after I finish talking with your mother.

MRS. GOLDMAN: Sit down. She'll be right with you. You did very good today. Getting back to what you were saying—*(softly)* you mean that a deaf person can get all of their hearing back with this operation?

The conversation continues, but the voices trail off so that the audience has trouble hearing what the women are saying.

DR. SNYDER: *(softly)* Well, a lot of it. At least, that's what the otorhinolaryngologist claims.

MRS. GOLDMAN: *(softly)* The who?

MICHAEL'S MIND VOICE: For all the things you two are saying about me, I must look like wallpaper . . . you'll discuss my future, my speech, what colleges I should go to, the subject I should major in, blah, blah, blah.

DR. SNYDER: *(softly)* The otorhinolaryngologist. The ear, nose, and throat doctor.

MRS. GOLDMAN: *(softly)* I see. And how is this ear implant different from a hearing aid?

DR. SNYDER: *(softly)* It doesn't amplify sounds like the hearing aid he's wearing. Instead, sounds are transformed into electric pulses, and these pulses directly stimulate the auditory nerve fibers. It will be major surgery, requiring general anesthesia. Lately, the surgeons have gotten the time down to two to three hours. It used to be an eight-hour operation.

MICHAEL'S MIND VOICE: *(to an imaginary audience)* My speech, my speech, my speech. Wanna hear what it's really like? Supercalifragilisticexpialidocious . . . see?

Michael goes to the table as if appreciating the audience's response to his fingerspelling performance.

MRS. GOLDMAN: *(softly)* What happens during the operation?

DR. SNYDER: *(softly)* What they do is shave the hair from the scalp about four inches up from the ear—wait—let me grab a diagram. *(gets a diagram)* They make a wide C-shaped cut on the scalp and pull back the flap to uncover the skull.

MICHAEL'S MIND VOICE: I say it perfectly, in my mind that is . . . isn't that what matters?

DR. SNYDER: *(with full voice)* A hole is drilled through the bone—this is so the doctor can fasten the electrode to the cochlea. Here's where the hole will be drilled. Are you all right, Mrs. Goldman?

MRS. GOLDMAN: Uh, yes, no.

The doctor helps Mrs. Goldman sit down.

DR. SNYDER: Put your head between your knees for a minute. You'll feel better.

MICHAEL'S MIND VOICE: Thank you very much. Thank you. Please, all of you sit down.

DR. SNYDER: Can we go on?

MICHAEL'S MIND VOICE: I'm extremely flattered . . .

DR. SNYDER: Okay, here's the cochlea where the electrode will be fastened.

MICHAEL'S MIND VOICE: I've got tears in my eyes . . .

DR. SNYDER: A micro-receiver and battery will be permanently cemented to his skull just above the ear.

MICHAEL'S MIND VOICE: Please stop . . . Thank you . . . *(to the women)* Why can't you just let it go? . . . leave me be . . . I wanna go home and work on my old truck . . . nothing like working with Dad and having him teach me about how all the parts work.

> *Michael takes out his knife and starts fooling with the plug on the broken lamp. He fixes the plug to make a better connection.*

MICHAEL'S MIND VOICE: I still can't believe Dad got it for 50 bucks . . . a '48 Chevy Pick-Up . . . original engine parts . . . only 64,000 miles . . . and what's it need? . . . a paint job . . . some new wiring . . . a new generator . . . some fenders . . .

> *Michael's Mind Voice goes down and the women's voices come up.*

DR. SNYDER: A tune up of the implant device must take place about six weeks after surgery when the incision has healed. The tune-up is like starting up a computer.

MRS. GOLDMAN: What about the success rate?

DR. SNYDER: It's been very good–about 75 percent. If the operation isn't successful, he wouldn't lose much anyway.
Maybe a slight balance problem, that's all. Anyway, it's a
very good gamble. When they were experimenting on mon-
keys and cats . . . *(Her voice gets softer)* the success rate was
higher. Now considering Michael's profound hearing loss. . .

MICHAEL'S MIND VOICE: . . . geez, all cosmetic bullshit . . .
WOOO! 50 bucks . . . this is going to be my life's work . . .
I don't have to talk to a truck or lipread its body parts . . .
just enjoy what I got and do it . . . hate it when people add
fancy whistles, bells, and flashers on their old vehicles
instead of keeping its original shape . . . this would do it . . .
Hey, Snyder . . . I can't believe you didn't get this fixed for
a whole year.

*Michael plugs in the lamp and turns it on. He plays with
the drawstrings turning the lamp off and on.*

DR. SNYDER: Michael! How did you do that?

Michael holds up his knife.

DR. SNYDER: Well, I know the knife didn't do it all. I don't
know how to thank you. I'm embarrassed to say I was too
lazy to get that thing fixed.

MICHAEL: 'Kay. I wanna go home.

MRS. GOLDMAN: We'll be going home soon. Sit down. Dr.
Snyder wants to tell us something very important.

MICHAEL: Whuuhh?

MRS. GOLDMAN: I don't like your tone of voice. We'll explain in
a minute.

DR. SNYDER: I was talking with your mother about a new hearing device that will probably be wonderful for you.
Wouldn't you like to work with something better than the
old body aid? *(no response from Michael)* Look at me. You

would be an excellent candidate for it. No more straps. No more lugging around that weight or messing with the wires.

Michael does not respond.

MRS. GOLDMAN: What do you think, Michael? Do you understand? It's a great idea.

DR. SNYDER: And, oh, you're going to love this part—you won't ever have to take your hearing aid batteries out at night to recharge them. Never again.

MRS. GOLDMAN: *(starts to gesture)* You'll love this—never will have to recharge your batteries again.

MICHAEL: *(pause)* Really?

As Dr. Snyder explains the procedure to Michael, Mrs. Goldman gestures and rephrases the doctor's sentences at the same time.

DR. SNYDER: *(more demonstrative)* Yes, indeed. Now, here's what we have to do. We will have to do a little operation inside your ear. You will be asleep, of course, and we will put in a tiny, little hearing aid—even smaller than President Reagan's—that will last you the rest of your life.

MRS. GOLDMAN: You will be asleep . . . they will put in a tiny little hearing aid . . . smaller than President Reagan's . . . lasts forever.

MICHAEL: Yeah? How?

Dr. Snyder and Mrs. Goldman speak at the same time.

DR. SNYDER: First, the doctor will put you to sleep. Then, the nurse will shave your head about, oh . . . about four inches above your ear . . .

MRS. GOLDMAN: Doctor will put you to sleep . . . the nurse will shave some of your hair above your ear and—

MICHAEL: What?

MICHAEL'S MIND VOICE: Whoa.

MRS. GOLDMAN: She said the doctor will put you to sleep and the nurse will shave your hair above your ear—

MICHAEL'S MIND VOICE: No! You will not . . .

MICHAEL: Nah!

MICHAEL'S MIND VOICE: Take my hair off, no!

MICHAEL: Nah!

MICHAEL'S MIND VOICE: No tape, no way, you're not going to strip my hair.

MICHAEL: Nah!

MICHAEL'S MIND VOICE: From my skin—no!

MRS. GOLDMAN: Michael, calm down, hon.

MICHAEL: Nah!

MICHAEL'S MIND VOICE: You will cut a hole . . .

MICHAEL: Don't want that!

MICHAEL'S MIND VOICE: . . . in my ear . . . no! . . . leave me be . . .

MICHAEL: Nah! . . .

MICHAEL'S MIND VOICE: Leave me be . . . I'm fine the way I am . . .

MICHAEL: This who I am!

MICHAEL'S MIND VOICE: You're not taking my hair . . . not from my skin . . . .

MICHAEL: Nah!

DR. SNYDER: Michael, we're not doing this yet, just talking about it. Your mother is very interested and I have to admit, this will make your life so much more profitable for you.

MRS. GOLDMAN: This is very important, now listen!

DR. SNYDER: Sit down, Michael. I'm not finished.

Michael moves to sit down but breaks away just before he sits.

MICHAEL and MICHAEL'S MIND VOICE: *(together)* Nah!

MICHAEL'S MIND VOICE: Leave me alone you old bitch.

MICHAEL: I wanna go home!

MICHAEL'S MIND VOICE: What strange ideas are you putting in my mother's head?

MICHAEL: Home! Home!

MRS. GOLDMAN: Michael, don't disappoint me! Sit down.

MICHAEL: Why?

MRS. GOLDMAN: Sit down, young man. If you don't cooperate I'll have your father sell your truck. *(silence)* That's my boy. As I was saying before, we haven't made a definite decision about this operation. I need to discuss it with your father before we decide. Once he hears about it he'll probably be very happy to learn what a cochlear implant will do for you. Now I want to talk with Dr. Snyder about a few more details and then we'll go home. Okay? Smile. Now Dr. Snyder, suppose we go with this but later move out of Baltimore. What would we do about check-ups and parts that you talked about?

DR. SNYDER: You will be glad to know that there are 24 centers in the country that work with cochlear implants. If and when you move . . .

> *Dr. Snyder's voice fades, but she continues to talk in silence. Radio music and announcer's voice come up. Michael sits quietly. Without the women noticing, he pulls out his knife and slides a blade out. He stands and looks at the women talking. He feels the pull of the mind voice away from them and towards the table. He goes to the radio and unplugs it. The radio announcer's voice, radio tube lights, and booth light all go off. Michael cuts off the plug and drops it in his shirt pocket. He puts away the knife and goes back to his seat.*

RADIO ANNOUNCER: *(Ad-libbing may be necessary in order for the voice to cut off at the time Michael pulls the plug)* . . . every Friday afternoon. Next Friday our line-up will include famous Johns—I won't tell you who they are yet. Oh, ha-

ha, and of course, my name won't be on the line-up, ha-ha-ha. If you can guess the line-up of Johns by Thursday, you will win the latest compact disc technology from Bang and Olufsen. Again, our number is—

MRS. GOLDMAN: Thank you very much for such important advice. I know we went over our appointment time. I hope we haven't thrown you off your schedule.

DR. SNYDER: Not at all. It's my pleasure. Do discuss this thoroughly with your husband and call me when you decide. We'll make an appointment with the otorhinolaryngologist. You take care, Michael. Remember—look up five words a day.

(no response)

Michael and Mrs. Goldman exit. Michael's Mind Voice stays behind and watches Dr. Snyder. She plays with her recently fixed lamp, appreciative of what her patient did for her. She straightens up the table, and turns up the radio. She finds it's not plugged in. Next, she discovers that the plug is gone. Lights slowly fade to black; the ON AIR light snaps off.

Lisa Fay

❖❖

Lisa Fay graduated from Framingham State College in 1978 with a degree in Liberal Studies. Her education included a semester in London. She is involved with many community activities in Boston, where she has lived for the past ten years. Fay is on the board of directors for two housing groups working toward preservation of affordable housing and is a member of two writing groups—the Boston Writer's Union and the Women's National Book Association. In 1989, Fay won third place in the Cambridge River Writing Competition. She also makes stained glass windows and has had her work exhibited at Boston's John Hancock Hall and at the Boston Public Library. Fay has had a severe bilateral hearing loss and cerebral palsy since birth.

Albert Einstein

When you were young,
the world clocked you slow,
while your mind raced faster
than light.

You broomed your family aside
to nurse numbers,
schooling yourself in a vacuum.

Your backroom numbers
groomed the Bomb for
pushbutton kids,
the equation easy
on any schoolboy tongue
but hard on peace.

You didn't want Germany
to host the Bomb;
Hitler gassed your homeland
so you coached Roosevelt
to smoke Hiroshima and Nagasaki.

The world never sleeps,
her dreams blink yellow.

Lisa Fay
73

My Yankee Friend

Though we are more than 50 years
we are close as cells
bubbling with mortal memories
to be immortalized
by me, a mere poet—
a tall order
on short notice.

You sweep me through the century
better than history books
living from the Spanish-American War
to Kuwait,
still ticking for peace.

The painting of your contemporaries
at the Museum of Fine Arts:
Degas, Monet, Cassatt, Matisse
hang for the critics
while we enjoy Cassatt
with our tea.
You saw Isabella at the Symphony.
"She was never a phony,"
you'd say.

You skipped the Depression,
hopping to Honduras
where five maids doted on you
while your friends starved.
Your unfaithful husband
drove you back to Boston
where you worked
when it was a whisper.

Lisa Fay
74

You never complained
you got with it,
sat in stiff back chairs
with crooked fingers
typing on cranky typewriters
and did it.

You now gallop two miles
to errands, lunch hours, and meetings
as though it were next door.
Though more than 50 years younger,
I run to meet your horsy gait.
On one of your gaitly walks,
you stopped me in the street
to let me know
always let manners show.

Subway Conductor

One wintry night
among a subway crowd
of recession faces
a homeless conductor
waves his dirty artistic hands
into the unrecognized face
of a horn player
who blasts perfect music
to keep him away from life.

Upstairs from Park Street station,
a producer stirred by Billboard talent
gallops downstairs buzzing with sirens.
With Mother Teresa's heart,
the producer slips a $100 bill
in the conductor's pocket
before police house him
at Pine Street Inn.
The player leaves him,
winking.

Lisa Fay

Raymond Luczak

Raymond Luczak (the *c* is silent) became deaf at the age of seven months, due to double pneumonia. After graduating from Gallaudet University, he moved to New York City. His play *Snooty* won the New York Deaf Theatre's 1990 Sam Edwards Deaf Playwrights Competition. Later that year, his essay "Notes of a Deaf Gay Writer" was featured in *Christopher Street* and was reprinted in *Deaf Life*. A chapter from his novel *A Collage of Hands* appears in *Men on Men 4* (1992, NAL/Dutton). Luczak, who is a native of Michigan's Upper Peninsula, is the editor of the anthology *Eyes of Desire: A Deaf Gay and Lesbian Reader*, to be published by Alyson Publications in Spring 1993.

Learning to Speak I

Mary Hoffman, didn't you know what you had
done when you drove all the way from Ramsay, those
photocopies sitting beside you in
your car?

       Your long blonde
hair, thin fingers, a tiny waist and eyes that
lit up at how I'd imitated signs off
your hands as we turned over the page for the
next sign, an arrow
indicating how I should whoosh right through the
air, my palms flat like airplane wings and yet so
coordinated with my mind, buffeted by
     seeing Ironwood's
     only deaf man, Gramps.

               He worked evenings at
Hurley's Holiday Inn, in its kitchen where
he was dishwasher. Afternoons he sat in
front of the bar near
Santini's Gift Shoppe, his hands folded on
lap until one kid or two came with their hands
fingerspelling their names or something until
     he smiled, or laughed. He
would then fingerspell, slowly, so that they could
understand it. I stared at his lips, hardly
moving.
        I thought how I hated my voice, the
        faces everyone
        in my class made when I tried to explain what
        I had meant: why couldn't I just sit there like him,

Raymond Luczak
78

not having to say anything? I sneaked
into the public
library and found some old sign language books.
I took them home, hiding them in my Jacquart's
burlap bookbag and reading them upstairs where
no one would catch me
trying arrows, wriggles and stillness on the
bed. Sometimes I'd hear quite suddenly the click
of the downstairs door opening—I'd slam my
book shut and cover
it with something else so no one would ever
think I was learning to be Gramps in secret.
And I rather liked the blue Deaf-Mute Cards he'd
passed

      out. One found its way
home: our kitchen table. I picked it up, piqued:
who was that man, smiling with ears sticking out?
"My name . . . GRAMPS, a Deaf-Mute . . . Thank you so
much for
your kindness." Handshapes
showed how A to Z could be formed; I wondered
how this contraband piece was smuggled in, and
left just so with Mom kneading dough right next to
it. I stared, thinking:

                Does it mean I'm allowed to learn? I learned it
                anyway. The handshapes fit naturally,
                easily. It got so I practiced running through
                everyone I
                knew until their names were wrapped over on my
                fingers.

                Late at night I dreamed of a voiceless
                world, where everyone signed and understood me.
                Lipreading would be banished, or at least,
                expectations of me
                having to lipread. I longed to be more deaf,

mute like Gramps who sat in front of
Hulstrom's and
waved when I sped by
on my ten-speed bicycle.

I wanted to
stop, to see his eyes take me along with
those earmolds that stuck out like his ears under
his baseball cap. I
wanted not to have to say anything, to
isolate myself from the rest of them, the
boys who laughed at my nasal speech, Father
K's silent gazes,
and the teachers' apologetic looks. Well,
if I couldn't hear as well as they, I thought:
Might as well learn.

So Mom told me then, that
you would come in our
house to teach me what you knew. They seemed
resigned,
as if they'd expected I'd learn it anyway.
You came frequently, and then you called Mom to
        apologize, I
can't come today. She told me later you had
multiple sclerosis. I couldn't see you
in my mind: your fingers frozen, unable to
lift?

The next time you
came, you only said, Sorry, I was sick, and
opened to where we'd stopped the last time. Then
came the day I *knew*, that I wouldn't see you
again, not for a
long time.

Later I took to riding into
town and seeking Gramps on his bench. I parked my
bike beside where he sat, and talked for some time.
We fingerspelled to

each other as passersby shook their heads at
us, *deaf people:* look how they can talk without
voices!

Mary Hoffman, didn't you know what
you had begun when
you agreed to teach me my first, and then, the
next sign until I couldn't stop, not until
I became Gramps, not mute but raging instead,
hands howling volumes?

Mrs. Kichak's Plum Tree

The tree never grew large.
Its two-inch thorns cast shadowy needles
in winter. No one went near.

But came autumns when I stole
its plums, big as robin's eggs.
I bit into them behind our shack

where bittersweet juice dribbled
out of my mouth's corners.
Crime had never tasted so sweet.

How its embittered bark fell
in angry chips every autumn
all over the soft tufts.

The Audiologist

The thick gray windows never reveal
her shadowy figure. The audiologist
always has something to conceal
behind those windows. She only reveals
to Mom how I did this year. I steal
a look at my audiogram and her checklist.
The thick gray windows never reveal
her shadow figure: the audiologist

and I are at war
over my ears, my headphones, my chair.
First she makes a beep, or a low roar—
and then I'm at war
with myself. Did I truly hear
that or not? My hand shoots up in the air,
volleying against her score
over my ears, my headphones, my chair.

The thick walls absorb my silence.
I cannot hear anything from outside,
except through my ear-burning, tense
headphones. They absorb her silence.
I wrestle with my ears, my conscience,
as I close my eyes to listen, decide.
The thick walls absorb my silence
as her sounds come from the other side.

Raymond Luczak
83

Practice

I stared at the black telephone
in Grandma's house
a bike ride from home

The receiver drooped like a brick
as I watched the slow wheel
whir back into place to "0"
after each number I dialed

In the dining room
I held it upside down
near my body aid

Exposed for the occasion

I stared at the kitchen
almost warped linoleum floor
a yellowing white

And waited
a loud ring then three ripples

Then a man's voice said Hello

Hello
        Hello?
                I stared
at the lid of holes
choked with brown dust

This is Ray

Raymond Luczak
84

Oh Ray   Raymond   This is Dad

I squinted at the smooth tear
under Grandma's old chair

   Dad

Yes yes   you understand me
This is so great
How are you doing over there

I wondered what kind of things
would he say on the telephone

It's hot here

He laughed   It's hot here too

   I never heard his laugh so
   close in my ears

Ray   you ready for your word

Yeah

Okay here we go   Superman

What

Superman

I closed my eyes   What

Superman   Su per man

Raymond Luczak
85

What

Superman   Su per man   Superman   you know
It's a bird   it's a plane   it's Superman

It's a word   I know that

Superman   Can you understand me

I thought   No why do I have to practice

What is it now

        It's Superman   It starts with a S

Stupid man   That's not one word   That's two words

No Ray   Listen   Listen now   Superman
He's from the comics

The receiver turned hot in my hand
finger bleeding with sweat

I don't understand   Dad

No   Try one more time   Superman   Su per man
He flies like Peter Pan

Duperman   Beaterman   That doesn't sound like a word
        Super man   Superman   Ray

I stared at the cradle

        Well I   I can't understand you

Raymond Luczak

Okay   Bye bye now

I wished

my body aid alone
on the kitchen floor
smash

                    smash it
with the receiver

A Wish, Unheard

Once I saw him sitting in his crowded office from a new distance.
Coworkers were laughing, giggling almost, beside his huge window:
a view of the world grew shimmering through the morning glass.
There were the usual skyscrapers, throngs of shoppers, impatient cars.
As with anything else, he'd ceased to notice; it had always been his.
He doubled over in laughter while others tossed in more jokes.
He did not have to lipread or ask for a rewind: I wanted to sliver
off my ears—forgetting I could catch only so much—and
give him my bloodied ears on a satin pillow and say,
Here. All this is my life.

The Finer Things

Michael is wandering the circular hallways of the Hirschhorn Gallery of Art when he notices an older man with a thick blond beard, wearing a pair of olive corduroys and burgundy Weejuns. Michael looks away, wishing he didn't always have to explore art museums alone and be pursued by one man or another on Saturday afternoons. He knows other men seem to admire his own rust-colored beard and the shape of his ass, but his lover Tom had said he could never be patient enough to sit and stare at paintings the way Michael did. He moves on to the next sculpture, which appears to be made of long copper toothpicks; it looks like it's torn between two skewered fences. He does not note the name of the sculptor; he is feeling somewhat hot and hard because the man keeps glancing back now and then; he keeps thinking, If he smiles again, I'm cooked.

He turns his hearing aids back on, just in case the man approaches him; when alone, he has no need for sound or noise. He always forgets how loud the groans of the Metrobus can be when it passes, or how incessantly babbling a crowd of people can be. Besides, turning off the hearing aids helps him concentrate on the painting in front of him and ignore the squeals of children pointing out this and that on the wall.

The next time he looks, the man smiles openly. He chuckles somewhat at Michael's apparent embarrassment, and strides over. "What do you think of this sculpture?"

Michael looks up, surprised by how tall the man is and how hazel his eyes are. Their color reminds him of golden maple leaves turning brown. "I'm sorry?" He asks as he turns up the volume on his hearing aids.

"Oh. . . ." The man points to his own ear. "Can you hear me?"

"Yes. Just say it again."

"I was asking, What do you think of this work?"

"Oh." Michael looks at it. "It doesn't make any sense."

"Then what are you doing here?" The man laughs easily.

Michael drops his shoulders. "I don't know."

"Were you hoping for someone like me?"

"I have a lover."

"He doesn't try to understand you? Or this?"

Michael laughs nervously.

"Come on now." The man places a hand on Michael's shoulder. "What's your name?"

"Michael."

"Ah, Michael. I'm Alec." As they shake hands, Michael notices how moist his palms are. "Mind if we go outside? I need to smoke."

From their bench, Michael can see a panorama of tourists walking mostly towards the Washington Monument to see the cherry blossoms on the Tidal Basin. In two months he will graduate with a bachelor's degree in graphic arts from Gallaudet University; he's not sure where in this city he could find a job in his field. Despite the importance of graphic arts in the media, he has heard that no one almost ever finds a job in their major, even in 1988.

"Michael, I don't know if you've seen me around before, but I've noticed you in other museums and galleries."

"You have? Where?"

"Up at the Corcoran. You seem to like postcard reproductions of Caravaggio and Raphael a *tremendous* lot."

Michael's jaw drops.

"Yes." He chuckles. "And I was so *pleased* to see you again because it's not often I see someone so young just standing there so patiently in front of some collage, or some painting." He inhales from his cigarette. "Tell me, what are you studying now?"

"Graphic arts at Gallaudet."

"Wasn't that great, with all that coverage on the student protest for a deaf president? I'll bet you were thrilled when King Jordan won."

"Yeah. He's still trying to get used to being the top dog on campus. So we just move on and do what we must do."

He shakes his head. "But don't you ever study art itself? Art history? Literature? Things like that . . . . You have such a fine nose. Would you know how I'd paint that? I'd paint it simply like. . . ."

"Like Van Eyck?"

"Yes! But tell me, why are you taking graphic arts when you should be at the Corcoran?"

"I don't know. Never heard of any art school until I came here."

"Really? Why haven't you heard of it before?"

Michael points to his ears. "Reason enough for you?"

"No." He exhales smoke meditatively. "I'm trying to think of any great artist who was deaf, and all I can think of is Beethoven. You do know his work?"

"Never heard his music." Michael shrugs.

"Oh, you *must* hear him! What about Mozart?"

"Who?"

"What are they teaching you over there? Andy Warhol?"

"No . . . but I happen to like some of his Pop Art."

"What he's doing is a total insult to the standards of art! It's not Pop Art, it's Slop Art!"

Michael is surprised to see that anyone could be so vehement over Warhol, or over any artist for that matter.

"Why?"

"Now all the young artists think they don't need mastery of any craft to pass for art, true and genuine art! It's supposed to take years and years before someone dares to call himself an artist. You know, I'm not terribly fond of either modern or contemporary art."

"I guess I'm different from you." Michael is surprised at

how much he wants to push Alec a little more—and he is really a total stranger, come to think of it—just to hear more of his opinions. "I like modern art."

"Watch what terms you use. You just don't throw them around like. . ."

"Like nerf footballs?"

"Yes." He laughs. "Yes! I hope you do know the difference between modern and contemporary art?"

"Modern art is by those who worked and died in this century, contemporary is by those who are still working and living in this century."

"Ah. I like that." Alec smiles and looks at him.

"Shall we have dinner at a restaurant I know in Georgetown? I'll pay."

Alec ushers him into L'Escargot and leads him to a table near the back of the restaurant. Michael feels awkward among the many tables covered with immaculately white tablecloths and so many wine glasses with triangularly folded napkins resting neatly inside. They walk past cream-colored candles in shiny brass holders waiting on empty tables to be lit; Michael is not sure what to do with his old denim jacket. Alec takes it without saying a word, hangs it on the coathook behind him, and gestures with his open palm that Michael should sit opposite him.

Alec lights another cigarette and says, "I know the owner so I get the best table here. You like it?"

Michael looks around and looks at himself, suddenly embarrassed over his appearance. He is wearing an old shirt, Levi's, and a pair of black Converse basketball sneakers.

"I—I've never been in a fancy place like this."

"No one ever uses the adjective *fancy* anymore. This is an *upscale* place for people who do know how to appreciate the finer things of life."

"The finer things of life?"

"Yes. Great art. Great food. Great classical music. Listen."

Alec leans over to one side. "Can you hear that?"

Michael turns up his hearing aids again. The music seems florid with piano keys twinkling among violins.

"A little."

"That's Ravel. He's a French composer. Have you ever heard 'Bolero'?"

"What?" He feels embarrassed.

"Michael. Do you want to learn about the finer things of life? Don't you and your lover want to live around here? Look, where are the galleries?"

"Dupont Circle. And sometimes Adams-Morgan. Where else?"

"Right. Don't you want to live like these people?"

Michael remembers walking the streets of Dupont Circle and Georgetown in the year when he first moved here. He peered at the walls behind lit windows; they always seemed filled with hardcover books and almost always a painting or two on the opposite wall. He dreamed often of taking his cold and wet shoes off those nights and wriggling his toes in the desert heat of their fireplaces and then pouring over all those art books. He finally says, "I don't know any deaf people who live like you."

The waiter comes around. *"Et quelque chose à boire, peut-être?"*

"I don't know." Michael looks helplessly at Alec.

"Je pense q'une bouteille de votre Bordeaux préférée—peut-être 1978—fait du bien, n'est-ce pas?"

"Oui, monsieur."

When the waiter leaves, Michael leans over. "What was that?"

Alec laughs. "You are going to taste some *wonderful* wine, my dear. Now, tell me," Alec opens his laminated menu, "have you ever tried escargots?"

"What?" Michael is still dazzled by the prices in the menu and the fact that all of the dishes have French names, without any explanation of what they contain. Worse yet, he doesn't know how to pronounce anything in French when the waiter returns for their orders.

"Look." Alec's fingernail points to the Premiers Plats section, and drops down to the word *escargots*.

"Never heard of them."

"What? You must try a few. They're delicate, but oh so delicate."

"But what are they?"

"They're snails cooked in a buttery sauce."

"Snails? Do you eat the shells, too?"

"Oh God no. Just wait and see." He chuckles. "Mind if I order what I think would be an exquisite introduction to French gourmet cooking?"

"To French what?"

"Gourmet cooking."

"What's that?"

"Haven't you ever heard of 'gourmet'?"

"No. Could you spell it out?"

"G-O-U-R-M-E-T."

"Gour-met?"

"No. You say it the French way. Gour-may."

"Gour-may?"

"Yes. Gourmet."

"Gourmet."

"There. You got it. Don't you have some special teacher showing you how to say all those wonderful words?"

"No. I never met a speech therapist who was into gourmet cooking."

He laughs, but stops. "Are you really that deaf?"

"Sometimes."

"But you don't seem to need sign language."

"I can't live without it."

"Why not?"

"It's just a part of me." He hated speech therapy even more

when he saw how much easier it was to converse with his hands. It felt so natural, so *of-course*.

"But what about this artistic part of you?"

"That's the hearing part of me."

"The what part of you?"

"Hearing. You're hearing. I'm deaf."

"Oh, so that's what deaf people call normal people—"

"I don't like that term."

"What term?"

"'Normal.' Hearing people are not normal when they think they are better than deaf people."

Alec's face flickers briefly as he extinguishes his cigarette into an ashtray. "I didn't mean to suggest . . . I'm very sorry if I offended you."

"It's all right. Really."

"You know what just occurred to me? No finer thing is ever normal, and so I intend to banish that word from my vocabulary right now. But you must remember, if you want to appreciate the finer things of life, you can't bend so low you forget what art is all about."

"Right. What would you say is the point of art?"

He chuckles. "You are a sharp cookie."

"'Sharp cookie'?"

"It's just a phrase. You know, like . . . "

"'Raining cats and dogs.'"

"Oh God. That's an old idiom."

They watch the waiter open the Bordeaux and pour a sparkling trickle of wine into Alec's glass. He sniffs and tastes it, swishing the wine in his mouth for what seems minutes. He nods; the waiter pours and leaves. Alec pats the back of Michael's hand and indicates they should both hold their glasses up in the air.

"Cheers."

"Cheers?"

"It's a standard greeting. A toast."

"Oh. Cheers."

"Ah." Alec smiles before he sips from his glass. "Just superb."

Michael sips. The wine tingles along his taste buds and down his throat. He feels slightly hot, as if in a fever but not quite, and a flush comes over his ears.

"What do you think?" Alec asks.

"I don't know."

"You must learn to determine and give opinions. An opinionated man is much more intriguing. And that is the point of art."

"What is the point of art?"

"A well-crafted statement, pure and simple. Tell me, what do you think of the wine?"

Michael thinks about what would be an appropriate statement, a good opinion: "It's light as a summer rain."

Alec claps his hands together and holds them to his lips. "Michael. That is beautiful. It makes me wonder why you're with a lover who doesn't do the things you want to do the most."

"I don't know. He's deaf-blind."

"Deaf . . . blind? So he can't see art the same way you do."

"No. But I think he sees it in a very different way than we do."

"How so?"

"People rely too much on their ears and eyes. He relies on his nose, and he could tell you just about anything by smelling."

"But what does his nose have to do with art?"

"Isn't art supposed to be a complete experience?"

"I wish . . . Ohhh. I see what you mean. The nose is the most underrated of all our senses."

"Right."

"Well, I hope he appreciates your beautiful nose."

"In any case, great art should inspire all of our senses."

Michael feels his body trembling from making such a big statement; he somehow feels Alec will be able to ease that vague yearning inside him. There has to be something more to life than just a job, a lover, and a nice apartment.

"'Inspire' our senses? Don't you think *stimulate* is a better term?"

"'Stimulate'? What's the difference between 'inspire' and 'stimulate'?"

The waiter returns for their order. As Michael sips his wine, he tries to lipread the French flitting back and forth. Their voices seem like strains of a melody he has to hear more of. Alec smiles at him as he indicates the various dishes Michael should try. *"Merci bien."*

"What was that?"

"We were speaking French."

"I know, but what was that last thing you said?"

"Merci bien? That was 'thank you' in French."

"How do you say it?"

"Merci bien."

"Merci bine?"

"No. *Merci bien.*"

"Merci bien."

"Now you'll be able to thank Pierre when the meal is over."

"Pear?"

"No. Pierre. French for 'Peter.'"

"Oh, Pierre."

"So it seems you know a tremendous lot, but you've never heard things pronounced."

"Yes." Michael is pleased that someone else—a virtual stranger—could deduce that much about him. "What do you do for a living?"

"I write essays on art and film and I review biographies, that sort of thing, for a lot of magazines."

"Which ones?"

"Oh, you'd never have heard of them. They're just avant-garde."

"They're what?"

"Avant-garde. Different."

"I don't understand."

"I'll spell, it okay. A-V-A-N-T G-A-R-D-E."

"Oh. That's how you say it?"

"Yes. Avant-garde."

"Avant-garde."

"You got it right." Alec pauses. "Do you ever read *The New Yorker*?"

Michael looks about, a little lost.

"Michael, you can't not have heard of it!"

He feels hotly humiliated. No one told him he should read that; there were always so many things he wanted to read.

"Oh, you must read it! A lot of opinionated people write stuff for it every week. You'd love it. Look, I'll buy you a copy from the newsstand down around the corner."

"You don't have to—"

"Nonsense. Not enough people know how to appreciate art, and you are dying to soak it all up. You've given me a mission."

"A what?"

"A mission. 'I'm going to show you things you never dreamed existed.' Like that? That was from *Auntie Mame*."

"Auntie Mame?"

"Don't tell me you've never seen it."

"Is it closed-captioned?"

"I'm sorry?"

"I have this box that brings out the hidden captions of the dialogue if it's closed-captioned."

"Why should you worry about that when you can understand me just fine?"

"Movies are not made to be lipread. You are."

"Well, Rosalind Russell is wonderful. You really must see it sometime. Oh, I can't believe this. There's a million worlds awaiting you. I'll show them all to you, if you want."

"What kinds of things?" Michael feels a little tipsy. The wine is very good, he thinks. He must remember to ask Alec the name of it so he can ask for it the next time he goes to a restaurant with Tom.

"Do you ever listen to music?"

"Sometimes."

"Rock music?"

"Yeah."

"Oh dear. You don't know what you're missing."

"What am I missing?"

"Worlds!" Alec lights another cigarette. "It's a shame you should have to live with a lover who can't teach you the things you really want to know."

"But I love him. Very much." Michael lowers his eyes.

Alec places his hand on Michael's. "I'm sorry. To whom do you like to listen?"

"The Pretenders . . . The Police, the Who, the Beatles, the Beach Boys."

"At least there's still hope for you. You like to listen to classic contemporary music. That'll translate well into classical music."

"But I don't know if I can hear the quiet stuff."

"Don't worry. That kind of appreciation comes over a long time. Did you fully appreciate the Beatles the first time you heard them?"

"No . . . . I just liked 'Yellow Submarine' and went on from there."

"Ah, 'Yellow Submarine.' So you must have heard something so charming you had to explore the rest of what they did. Hmmm."

The waiter places two tiny plates of grilled escargots between the two men. Michael says, *"Merci bien."*

"Je suis étonné—votre français est parfait!" The waiter looks bewildered.

Alec laughs. *"Il ne connaît que 'Merci bien.'"*

The waiter looks relieved and leaves.

"What did you say?"

"I told him your French is limited to 'thank you.'"

"*Merci bien.* Oh, I speak such bad French."

Alec laughs as he takes his tiny escargot fork and pitches the tiny ball of meat out of the snail's shell. "Go on try it." He dips it into the sauce. "Mm-hmm. They did it just right, as usual."

Michael looks apprehensively at the escargot before he imitates Alec in dipping it into the sauce. He feels funny eating snail, but he is surprised at how good it tastes in his mouth. He is disappointed that there are only six snails left, and that each snail could contain so little.

"Ah. Now sip some wine. See how it affects your taste."

Michael's tongue feels suddenly bathed in a trickle of warmth. "It just feels different."

"That's the miracle of a great wine. You feel different."

"What?"

"Don't worry. You'll understand everything, all of what translates into the finer things of life. Here, have some more. He indicates the escargots. "You have so much more to learn. You have the nose for it."

"Stop talking about my nose!"

"I can't help it, it's so perfect." Alec gazes at Michael past the swaying candlelight. "May I touch it?"

As Michael feels the strange sensation of Alec's finger tracing the ridges of his nose, he thinks about his lover Tom. He realizes with a sudden pulse of pain that he and Tom have stopped exploring each other's bodies. When they'd first met, their hands and tongues were absolutely carnivorous, and now they just focused on the genitals.

"Why do you look so sad?"

"Oh, it's nothing."

"It's about him, isn't it?"

"Yes," he says with a sigh. "It's just not the same."

"People change. No one likes it when that happens. But change...that's the secret ingredient for great art."

"Secret what?"

"In-gree-di-ent."

"I'm sorry."

"I-N-G-R-E-D-I-E-N-T."

"Oh. The stuff that goes into food?"

He nods. "Michael, I take it you want to be an artist."

"Me? An artist? In what?"

"Anything you want. You should show me your portfolio sometime."

"Well, I've done some collages. . . ."

They look up as the waiter brings one dish after another to their table. "*Bon appétit!*"

"*Merci bien.*"

Alec tries not to laugh. "Did you truly understand what he said?"

"No. I just said thank you. I mean, what else can I say?"

"You're hilarious." Alec holds up his glass. "*Bon appétit.*"

"*Bon appétit?*"

"You got it."

As they sip their wine, Michael thinks again of Tom, who now must be wondering why he hasn't come home yet. How could he explain someone like Alec to Tom or to any of his deaf friends? They have never cared all that much about art; the looks on their faces loosened when they could talk about other things like Marlee Matlin or Gallaudet's newly appointed deaf president.

Michael tries a little bit of everything on Alec's plate and cleans his own. Everything is astonishingly delicious—he has never been so in love with any food before, and as he watches Alec sign the credit card slip, he thinks, I must go to Paris and try more of their food. The fullness of his stomach feels nice.

They walk in the twilight down to a magazine and book

shop on M Street, where Alec pulls a copy of *The New Yorker*. "This is for you."

Michael looks at the pastel colorings of its Roz Chast cover; he recognizes the magazine now, but he's never read it.

"Merci bien."

Alec laughs as he shakes his pack of cigarettes for another one. "So, you live off 16th Street?" he asks as he looks in the distance, where M Street splinters into Pennsylvania Avenue. If they walked a few blocks further over the P Street bridge, they'd be in Dupont Circle.

"I envy your lover, Michael. I really do."

"No, you shouldn't. I envy *you*, that you're able to know so much."

"Is it really that hard for deaf people like you?"

"What do you mean?"

"To appreciate art."

"Well, there's deaf culture. I suppose that's a different kind of art."

"Yes, it must be. Sign language has its own beauty. I thought I told you about when I saw the National Theatre of the Deaf perform a few years ago. But don't you want to learn more about art?"

"Well, I'm afraid of becoming so hearing I'll forget that I'm a deaf person."

"I don't think you'll forget. It just colors everything you do, that's all. When Beethoven became deaf, he wrote his greatest music. And all those blind musicians are so amazing. Oh God, I do want to kiss your nose."

"Not here."

"Do we have to go all the way to Dupont Circle just so we can kiss?"

Michael turns pink under the streetlight; they are ready to cross the bridge towards the subway station. "I've never had an affair before, and I don't want to get into the habit."

"Michael, have you ever been to New York?"

"No."

"You must. Tell you what. If I could take you up there next weekend, would you go?"

"What could I tell Tom?"

"Lie a little."

"I can't. I don't like to lie."

"Artists have had to lie now and then just to accomplish their work. You cannot be an artist without knowing what New York is like. You must meet as many New Yorkers as you can and hang around with people who appreciate the same things you do. Having them all in one place like New York makes creativity a lot easier than here in Washington."

"Then why do you live here?"

"The rent here is a hell of a lot cheaper. I go up to New York at least twice a month. Would you like to go? I'd be so happy to introduce you to a few gallery owners I know and just talk about art."

"Are they stuck-up? That's what I've heard."

"Whoever told you that? If they weren't friendly with people like you, they'd be out of business. They need something fresh, something original to stay in business."

"Oh. I never thought of that. But some galleries here don't seem to like having me around."

"You have to expect that. When they take a look at your clothes, they know you're either an artist or a window-shopper. And by the way, it'll help you a lot if you can dress better in New York."

"Artists are not supposed to make that much money."

"I know. But when you want to give a good impression, you have to bend a little. You know, I could stand here for hours and listen to the cars passing us by, and I'd be perfectly happy if I could be talking with you like this."

"Don't lie to me." He grins. "You said you wanted to kiss my nose."

"Yes, that too. That would make me so very happy. May I?"

Michael glances around. "I don't know. It has to be some-where else."

"You're welcome to my place." Alec kisses the tip of his index finger as if to say, This is how I want to kiss you—ten-derly.

"Could I have your phone number?"

"Gladly!" His hand darts in and out of his pockets until he finds a pen and plucks out his card.

"So are you thinking about coming to New York?"

Michael nods as he reads the card: Alexander A. Jonson.

"Would you understand me on the telephone?"

"You've been so easy to lipread so far, I can't imagine hav-ing a problem."

Alec watches the passing cars before he fixes his eyes on Michael's. "Can I have your number?"

"I don't think it's a good idea right now."

"It's all right. I understand. When can I see you again?"

"I'll call you."

"You're not one of those people who say that and never call?"

"Alec . . . I told you, I've never had an affair before."

"It's not an affair. Yet."

"I don't know if I can sleep with you."

"You're still in love with him?"

"Well, that's the problem. I don't know."

"Let's walk over to Dupont Circle. It's cold, but the air is very clear. You can see the stars."

In front of Tom's pink apartment building, Michael asks, "What time is it now?"

"Almost ten."

"Tom won't like this."

"Oh, I just don't have the heart to ask you again."

"My nose?"

"Yes."

Alec leans over and kisses his nose furtively and quickly.

"You know that's not enough for me." He slips a hand into his front pocket and pushes up his erection. "Now I have a problem here. I guess I have to go home and think of you instead. Please call me."

Tom is already sleeping when Michael comes in. Michael strips and slips into the cold place beside him. Tom reaches for the light and turns it back on. "Where-you all-day?"

Michael puts his hands under Tom's so Tom can read his signs. "Me-look-around H-i-r-s-c-h-h-o-r-n Museum, me-meet g-a-l-l-e-r-y o-w-n-e-r want see my work, maybe me-join ride New-York."

"New-York dangerous awful place, too-many muggings, won't g-o."

"Most artists live where-where then?"

"Here. You here."

"I-f you don't-want go New-York, me-go."

"Money where?"

"G-a-l-l-e-r-y o-w-n-e-r money have."

"O-h. You-like money? Himself gay?"

"Gay not-matter, want-want help me important."

"Slept-with-him finish?"

"Me-don't-like that. Me-thought you trust me."

"Me-48, you-22. You-young, not know do-do, horny a-l-l time, don't know how control, too-many people dying now."

"FINISH!" Michael signs and yells at the same time. He leaps out of the bed and stares at Tom signing to the air in front of him. He wants to weep because Tom doesn't know where Michael is in their tiny apartment, and he wonders who'd want to take care of Tom after he turns 49 next month. He pulls his clothes back on, and signs into Tom's hands, "You not-understand what me need life, my life."

"You young. Of-course."

"Not-like your-use my age excuse. You-want me-stay here, like jail. You not-want understand my-love art."

"That my fault?"

"We talk-talk same things over-and-over. Enough. Me-stay-with friend tonight. Me-come-back tomorrow."

"Me-thought you l-o-v-e love me."

Michael feels his eyes hurt with tears. "Me-love you but don't-know i-f enough for you."

Before he leaves the apartment, he dials Alec's number. He hears his answering machine and then, suddenly, a click. "Hello?"

"Alec?"

"Michael! Are you all right?"

"I need a place to stay tonight."

"You need money for a cab?"

"No I need to walk a bit first, just to clear my head."

"Absolutely."

"And one more thing."

"What?"

"No sex tonight, please."

"Oh . . . fine, fine. And, uh, can I ask you a favor?"

"What's that?"

"Bring along some of your work."

"My collages?"

"Of course!"

Michael walks to Alec's basement apartment on O Street, not far from the Dumbarton Oaks Gardens, and rings the bell. Alec is wearing a black-and-red velvet bathrobe as he opens the door to let Michael in. "I'm so sorry that you couldn't stay there tonight."

He looks around, and sees shelves of books everywhere. He looks at the shimmering parquet floor and treads across it gingerly, as if it is a glass sheet waiting to break.

"Michael, let me take your jacket. You can sleep on the sofa if you like."

"Thanks. *Merci bien.*"

Alec grins slowly. "Do you want to talk about it?"

"No. Not tonight."

"All right. May I look at your work?"

"Well, if you want." Michael watches Alec's face as he surveys each collage under the lamp.

"My God. Look at this. And you've never shown these?"

"No . . ."

"Why not?"

"I've never thought of myself as an artist."

"Doesn't the deaf community encourage you?"

"Well, not really. It's just that they've never really cared for art in the first place."

"Ah, I see. Do you want some tea or something?"

"Oh no. *Merci bien* anyway."

"You don't know how hilarious you can be. Oh Michael, you don't know it yet, but you are an artist."

"I'm not in the mood for heavy talk tonight."

"Okay." Alec brings out percale designer sheets and a goose-down comforter. "It's kind of cold here, but you should be warm. Of course . . . I think you'd be a lot warmer next to me."

"No *merci bien.*"

As Michael lies there watching the occasional headlights sweep through the front window, he wonders what kind of life he would lead if he were an artist. He gazes across the books on the shelves and wonders what kinds of things he would learn and what kind of person he would be if he could learn all the things Alec knows. Would he be so different that deaf people would not know what to do with him? Would they accuse him of being too hearing? Perhaps life would be easier for him in New York; he knew some deaf artists living there. And he would graduate in only two more months . . . .

He suddenly needs to pee. He wanders about carefully in the dark, and as he turns off the bathroom light, he can see Alec sleeping. He's left his bedroom door open. He steps in and notices that Alec's pectorals and lower arms are covered with feathery hairs. He wonders about Alec's age; he must be somewhat younger than Tom.

"Alec?" He whispers.

His eyes do not flicker. He comes closer to the edge of the bed, catches the scant moonlight illuminating Alec's nipples, and slips into bed next to him. Alec is indeed tired after all.

The next morning Michael awakens to find himself naked and Alec gone from the bed. He tries to remember whether they did anything, but he can't remember a thing. As he sits up, running his fingers through his hair, Alec appears with a breakfast tray. On it is a glass vase with a few marigolds and a porcelain teapot with a pair of matching cups quivering slightly.

"Good morning," he smiles. "You sit back."

Michael looks at the tuft of chest hair poking out of Alec's loose bathrobe. He piles the pillows behind himself against the headboard and unwinds his legs to accommodate the tray on his lap. "Did we do it?"

"Did we do what?"

"I don't know how it happened. I was wearing my turtleneck shirt and my underwear, and then . . ."

"Well, I don't know how you got into my bed. Michael, you were so incredible. I've never had anyone so responsive. You were just amazing."

"I'm sorry I don't remember anything. I'd have to see you naked."

"Later. You need some tea first."

"Tea? I hate tea."

"It's not the Lipton variety, mind you. Oh." He stops. "Can you understand me without your hearing aid?"

"I told you, you're very easy to lipread."

"Merci bien."

"What was that?"

"Ahhh." He shakes his finger. "I spoke a little French for

your benefit."

"*Merci bien?* God."

"This kind of tea is real and authentic." He takes the cover off the teapot. "See this? There are no tea bags. Real leaves, here." He pours some into their cups. "Try some. It's not too hot now."

Michael sips tentatively. The tea proves to be gentle without any acrid aftertaste.

"Like it?"

"Yes. Yes!"

"I want you to know that art is not just a painting or an object. Look at the wall paper there and the way those dressers complement it. That's a different kind of art, and boiling tea leaves is also an art in itself." Alec rests an arm on Michael's shoulders. "Making love is an art too, and you are among the best I've ever had."

"How many guys have you had?"

"Too many. Yeah. You leave them all out in the cold."

"Alec. You can't mean that."

"Yes, I do. And I want you to be the best artist you can be. I don't care what you think of your life right now, but you must go to New York."

"What about us?"

"Something as good as this can never last very long."

"Why not? What do you mean?"

Alec bites his lower lip. "Because. You will change. I have never seen anyone change so much in a mere twenty-four hours. You're changing already as I tell you this; I can see that in your eyes. You're going to be different; you are already different. Do you understand why?"

"You're saying this because you've just had me?"

"No. No. You're young. You have a whole world in front of you. No. Let me change that—you have more than one world waiting for you. As long as you are here, I'd be very happy to teach you all that I know. We can look at my art books and go to museums whenever we can. I can tell that you're not get-ting enough appreciation at your school, so, okay?"

"But, why? Why do you want to do all this?" The tea in Michael's mouth seems abruptly bitter; he puts his cup down on the tray.

"Because I am not an artist. Yes, I can talk about it. I can write about it, but I'm not the most honest critic in existence. I do not truly understand art as it is. Sometimes I make state-ments about art, but that's only because I want to fool myself and sound good to everybody else. I'm too afraid to live the life of an artist, someone who will keep asking questions that take forever to answer. You're not afraid to ask. That's why you're different from them and almost everyone else."

"What do you mean 'almost'?"

"Because there are so few people who—you don't have any pretensions. No one has told you how art should be, and yet I think you understand it better than I do. I have far too many pretensions; I'm stuck with them because I create them for a living. But you're free to find your own voice."

"I don't understand."

"Michael, I know. Look, you can see I live very well. But that doesn't mean I am a critic of the highest order. You are the first person I've met who's cut me down to size, and you didn't even know it! I can't be with you all the time, my entire sense of worth would be wiped out and what could I possibly have left?"

"Me," Michael says.

"Oh no." Alec bursts into tears. "You don't understand! What I'm trying to say is, you will be somebody."

"Ha. I don't even have a portfolio."

"You don't even need one. Those collages . . . No, it doesn't matter. You just have to keep working at it."

"But what about Tom?"

"Michael, I can't tell you what to do. Your passion for learn-ing, that is the finest thing of life any artist could even possibly ask for. Just listen to your heart, and ignore critics. Critics—like me—we're paid to con the public into thinking that by reading our reviews, they'll know art as well as we do. Tell me, who's your favorite art critic?"

"Well . . . I don't even know of anybody."

"That's the way it should be."

Alec looks at the Seth Thomas clock atop a lower dresser. "It's time for brunch. Oh come on, honey-nose, we've got to move on and figure out what we can do in New York."

As Michael walks beside Alec toward Dupont Circle, he sees in the distance two deaf men he knows. They are dressed in stone-washed jeans, L.A.-style T-shirts, and brand new denim jackets; their crew cuts stand on end, moist with mousse, and their moustaches are perfectly trimmed. They talk animatedly to each other and do not notice Michael walking beside Alec across P Street. He thinks about how the nights of these deaf men's lives will pass in bars, how they will age and adapt by changing bars. He remembers the awkward looks on their faces when they'd tried to talk with each other at deaf parties. Could he truly be that different?"

"You know them?" Alec glances back again.

"Yes," Michael says finally. "Once upon a time, but not anymore. I've got better things to look for."

Michael Winters

Michael Winters was born in 1943 ("too old to be a boomer") and raised in Oklahoma, Kansas, and Colorado. He moved to Texas after high school, where he earned a B.A. from Rice University. He has been a children's baseball, football, softball, and soccer coach; a gecko breeder; and elderly car mechanic; and—for nineteen years—a revenue agent with the IRS. Married nearly twenty-eight years, Winters has three children, two dogs, and lots of fish. He is chapter president of Self Help for Hard of Hearing People (SHHH) in Houston and editor of the local SHHH newsletter. Winters, who calls himself a frustrated writer, also plays golf, reads, collects fantasy and science fiction, and dreams of living in the mountains again. He has had a progressive hearing loss since the age of ten.

Melusine

Dawn slowed down over China and never reached Europe at all. Despite the missing sun, a dingy sort of light remained, as though all the world were inside an abandoned warehouse lit only by dirty skylights. This *should* have gotten everyone's attention, but too much else was going on.

Strangeness came at different speeds. Melusine Valdista, for instance, vacationing in the mountains of Italy, got a jump start. She hadn't been alone when she went to bed, nor terribly sleepy. But that had been last night, and on purpose. She'd expected to sleep late, certainly not to awaken in the dark, and least of all in the middle of a mob, made up mostly of men. Orgies she'd been to, but they weren't exactly what her psychiatrist had meant by "loosening up her life a bit." Particularly when she didn't know she'd been invited.

A common language would have helped her, but Melusine found that modern Italian wasn't it; nor was English nor what Spanish she still recalled. She watched uneasily as the strangers shouted mutually unintelligible phrases at each other, many reaching for swords and knives while arms waved everywhere. When Melusine spotted a few guns as well, she made a determined try for the door. The rest of the group joined in, and since the wall held, the narrow door let nobody out. A peek through the forest of hairy legs showed the futility of the attempt, the hall outside being just as crowded as her room. And since it didn't look as if the sun would rise and exorcise these ghosts (if that's what they were), or waken her from a bad dream (if *that* was the problem), Melusine gave up in disgust and headed back for bed.

Oddities were worldwide. In the Kremlin, Peter the Great objected strenuously to being told that he was no longer Tsar of all the Russias and being asked to kindly take his restored carcass back outside and into the ground where he belonged. Or at least, someone added, work out priorities with a couple named Ivan and Catherine. Fortunately for Peter, he found a number of troops from his guard handy, and actively disagreed. Before a mob made up of Napoleonic grenadiers, baggy-trousered Turks and Cossacks, and the odd Mongol tribesman, Peter proceeded to discover the hazards of debating terms with a squadron of tanks. Guns still blazing, he beat a hasty retreat, wondering among all his wonders why nobody seemed to have been hurt.

On the other side of the world, the current inhabitant of the White House, perhaps in an effort by parties unknown to create a certain balance, found himself engaged in a brisk discussion with a half-dozen or so of his predecessors, all the while hiding in the basement bomb shelter as a restored British fleet merrily shelled the modern city. Little help was available from the Court of St. James in the matter, due to a vigorous argument between Henry VIII and assorted wives, along with numerous other self-validated claimants to the same throne. The situation in places of more ancient lineage, such as China, while similar in overall nature, rapidly became indescribable.

And in another place, rather farther away, two parties found themselves unexpectedly sharing accommodations.

"Vishnu! What doth thee intend, thou reeking miscreant!

"Oh, skip the god-talk, Kulkulkan. There's nobody else around to impress!"

"Fine by me. By the way, what *are* you doing here? I distinctly recall locking up the place. If riffraff like you can get in . . ."

"Be damned to you too, buddy. This pit has two bedrooms, which you'd notice if you'd open your all-seeing eyes and exercise your all-knowing wits. Besides, you just hauled me off of the nicest piece I've had a chance at in years! I'm the one with the beef!"

"Beef all you want, cow-lover. I didn't drag your ugly self anywhere, least of all to my own . . ." The angry god trailed off as he looked around slowly. "Hey, where *is* this place? Looks primitive, like something you or Brahma might've done. Not anything I would have created."

"You feathered fink, bad as it is this dump's way too polished to be Mayan. You guys couldn't stack two bricks together without getting one of 'em crooked. But it's not ours and now that I look at it, I'm not sure who did do it."

"That's not all you're not sure about," said a third voice from the open doorway. "Step outside for a minute, friends. I think you'll have a surprise."

Vishnu and Kulkulkan followed the speaker into a hallway that wound about and faded vaguely off in both directions. Innumerable other doorways could be seen, most now opening to other bemused figures. Despite the seemingly indefinite length of the passage, they soon reached a great hall and crossed the tiled floor to a massive double doorway. Cronus gestured, then yawned mightily. The other two stared uncomprehendingly at the strange landscape; now that their anger had died down, they realized they were tired, as though they had just awakened from a very long nap.

"Cronus, do you have any idea what happened, or where this place is?"

"No, Vishnu, I don't. But I do know one thing," added the god of time. "A whole lot of time has passed since any of us were awake. Trust me to know that."

"You would," the others agreed.

Back on Earth, answers were in just as short supply. At a large state university, John Nolte, janitor and grad-student, leaned on his broom and looked dolefully out into the great courtyard. A sourceless grey light had descended here, as everywhere, though it should have been midnight by all rights. Behind him an irate voice raved on.

"Nolte, I demand some answers! What in the hell is going on out there?"

"Time's out of joint, I guess."

"Don't you quote Shakespeare to me, dammit! You're a physicist, not a blathering English major," shouted the president of the university.

"Dammit, I'm not God! There's just no way physics can explain this mess. Look outside, man! That's a bunch of Aztecs by the library, waving those bloody glass daggers. I'd hate to know where they found the blood. Over there, that's a mob of old Spanish soldiers shooting up the fountain. And Comanches are shooting back. And there, on top of the Admin building, that's a goddamned flying saucer! I can't tell if those clowns standing around it are even human, but they sure as hell look agitated to me. I don't know what any of them are doing or why they're here or when they'll go away!"

"Nolte, everyone else has disappeared. The Governor is sure to want some quick answers, and you better have some if you ever hope to get that doctorate! Answers, Nolte! Understand?"

"Yeah, Professor. I understand."

But he didn't, of course. For once, the little people knew every bit as much as the experts. Which is to say, nothing.

"It's alla them rockets, I tellya, Harry. Shouldn't let 'em go up no-ways. We wasn't made to fly in no space. Worse'na damn bomb tests!"

"Yeah," mumbled Harry around the neck of some muscatel. Good ol' Ernie, he always had things figured out.

Internal clocks ruled when mechanical failed. If it was light, it was time to work.

"Sure I see 'em, lady. Long as they stay outside on the street, er if they come in they got good money, whatta I care? I still gotta open up shop at seven, same as always. Now, do you wanna chop er not?"

Mrs. Gilmore sniffed in disdain at the costumed intruders marching down *her* street and returned her attention to Butcher Bob's suspect lamb. Most likely it's goat, she thought. Just wait till she told Elsie!

John Nolte stared out of the window. Physics hasn't an answer to this, he thought. The whole thing was impossible. He wished he'd taken a few courses in metaphysics, or religion; maybe they'd have some connection. "Yeah, that's it," he said to himself, "religion. Wonder if it's too late to join up?"

Religion didn't have the answer, but it certainly had a different point of view.

"In Odin's name, what's going on here?" roared Thor as he shouldered his way into the great hall. "This place is as crowded as a Swartalf torture chamber."

"Oh shut up, you northern fool!" snapped Zeus. "If I can't find out what's happening, it's a safe bet that you late-comers won't either!"

"Shut up yourself, Zeus," said Osiris. "Marduk and I were gods when you were living in a hole in the ground."

"Now, now," said Jehovah, "it's not how old you are, but how successful. So it's I that . . ."

"You've not been one bit more successful than I," screeched Allah, "and you've taken longer to boot. I'm the one who . . ."

"Who what?" asked the gravelly bass voice of Thunderbird. "Who caused this mess? If you did, I wouldn't admit it. There's a few of us who don't much appreciate this situation."

Ishtar pushed through the crowd of arguing deities towards the door, where Freya and Kali joined her. They stopped on the wide landing. Before them stretched league after league of tall grass—brilliant green blades waving in a gentle breeze. Small groves of trees were scattered at random, with a shadowed mass of wildwood crowning a low hill in the middle distance. Off to one side lay a sizable lake, with the sinuous forms of various marine gods and monsters splashing about on the surface, barely rocking a long flat boat with a single standing passenger. On the broad lawn in front of the main gate, a dark and stocky godling tossed a ball to an enormous, three-headed dog. Halfway around the horizon, a towering mass of pearly grey fog swirled in the distance, masking what might have been a hill to match their own. Far down the road assorted shapes were slowly making their way uphill. Other figures drifted about in the crystal-clear air.

"Who is that on the boat?" asked Kali.

"Charon. Says he's giving two-way rides now, but there aren't any passengers. And that's Gilgamesh playing catch with Cerberus. They don't know what the hell is going on either," said Thunderbird. "Don't plan on taking any long hikes, 'cause you can't. We're trapped here; even the sky is kind of low. Garuda and the Roc already smacked their heads against it. And you think it's crowded now! I can make out some angels coming, plus a bunch of Rakashah, some of the Tuatha de Danaan, and a lot I don't know. And there's even more beyond them!"

"It's not just here," said Kali. "You should see what's happening on Earth."

Down on Earth, situations were stabilizing, but normality was very little in evidence. Tsar Peter had finally wearied of being shot, even though it seemed to do him no permanent harm. He decided on a retreat to the seashore, so he set out for the nearest coastline. After considerable argument, he boarded a train for the trip.

The shelling died down at last on the Potomac, as the ships and weapons of the restored British fleet faded away. As unexpectedly as they had appeared, all anachronistic objects other than people and their clothes began to disappear. It was just as well; the recall of all humanity was taking up all the available space.

Melusine Valdista finally escaped both the mob and her room. Outside, the various linguistic groups were sorting themselves out of the mobs. Melusine found a small cluster of native English speakers halfway up a small hill just outside the village. Most were veterans of the last big war, but a few were young people, like herself. All were talking, few were listening.

"It's the Second Coming! God will set up His judgment seat and I'm not ready!"

"Bullshit. Ain't no such thing as God! This is just a dream, a bad trip, none of you are real. I got some bad hash, that's all."

"Nightmare, it's all a nightmare. What are we gonna do?"

"This is no dream," said a husky man in a World War II bomber jacket. Hitting Cassino from the air, *that* was a nightmare. Not this. But what has happened to my outfit? There's a war on!"

Melusine decided the tall pilot was just the sort of loosening up she could really get interested in; she sighed throatily in his direction. No one paid any attention, save one drab little man she hadn't noticed before. But the little man said nothing, he merely looked on with vague disapproval.

All over the world, the violence gradually stopped as people noticed that no injury was permanent. But, everyone was talking. And not just on Earth.

The various gods broke into groups, by specialty: sky gods on the balcony, fertility deities in the bedrooms, household gods about the fireplace. In the woods Pan and Krishna gathered a group of kindred spirits and threw a party.

Few of the gods possessed the attribute of patience, and many reacted spitefully on discovering the present situation called for nothing less.

Meanwhile, back on the now uniformly lighted Earth, the feeling of imminent catastrophe was gradually being replaced by the common sense wish to get on about the business of living.

Mrs. Gilmore, noting the street was now vacant, and much dissatisfied with both Butcher Bob's chops and his attitude, marched stoutly out the door. John Nolte, broom standing idly in the corner, continued calling churches, seeking one that would answer the phone. And on the Baltic beaches, Peter the Great discussed possible tactics with Gustav Adolph and Frederick-the-Also-Great.

Their discussion was duplicated in many places around the globe, in every spot where more than one notable personage congregated. But all talk gradually ceased, as it rapidly became obvious that no one else was paying the slightest attention.

Peter took it better than many of the famous. The prime ministers of various more or less democratic nations, with the presidents of others, recognized the faceless hordes from uncounted campaign rallies. Their urge to orate died slowly as they, too, saw total nonattention on all sides. But it was the movie and recording stars, the athletes and professionally daring, and others of the pampered and spoiled who collapsed in screaming fits of rage and tears. When even this attracted no attention, they settled in with all the rest to wait, wondering sadly what had happened to the media.

Melusine Valdista, as all men and women on Earth, looked uncertainly around at the many, many duplicates of the neutral little man she'd noticed earlier. The sound of simultaneous inhalation echoed around the globe. Everything else ground to a halt.

"I think," said Thunderbird softly, "that something is about to happen." The assembled gods and heroes watched as a single, smallish, quite unremarkable individual marched towards them. The little human was no more remarkable close up than he had been at a distance, except for his face, which looked as if countless multitudes of other faces were superimposed on it. The gods had little time to ponder before the small being, in perfect harmony with his millions of counterparts on Earth and with far more volume than even a god might have possessed, began to speak.

"Well, folks, the votes are all in. We've tried it the other way, now there's going to be a change. Forevermore the Law of Averages will be THE LAW! We'll see how all you special cases react to that!"

On Earth, the air and seas shook to the proclamation, simultaneously pouring from uncounted throats. Silence then reigned. The average man before the gods spoke again.

"No offense, but you'll soon have company. You can talk to them if you want. Meanwhile, it seemed appropriate to have all of you in the same place. And since we were doing that, why not let you wake up? Sorry for the inconvenience." And having said this, the man turned and walked away.

Thunderbird and those other of the deities blessed or cursed with farsightedness watched their visitor fade from their sight, long before the horizon was reached. Raising their gaze, they could see, perched on a new, visible duplicate of their own hill, another great conglomerated structure. Black asphalt roads wound up to this building, along which could be seen group after weary group, slowly making their way to their new home.

"Can anyone make out who they are?"

"I can, Ishtar," replied Thunderbird. "They're every king and prince and chief and notable the humans ever produced. If there are any ordinary citizens in that mob, they're in disguise."

And for the second time, Earth exiled its gods.

Trudy Drucker

Trudy Drucker is a medical and technical writer as well as a freelance poet/essayist. She received a B.S. cum laude from New York University, an M.A. summa cum laude from Fairleigh Dickinson University, and a Ph.D. with honors from New York University. In 1989, she retired as a full professor from Bergen Community College, where she had taught for twenty years. Her work has appeared in newspapers, lay and professional journals, and books, including *The New York Times*, the *American Association of University Professors Bulletin, The Christian Science Monitor*, and the *New York Herald Tribune*. Drucker has been moderately hearing handicapped since the age of five.

Sylvia

died with her head in the new poems
Like a good tinnitus
They roared for her over the gas hiss.

Mother who built the sea wall
muting the poems through the far water . . .
That roar was your real daughter,

that lady of babies and papers.
They scrape the spume
From her drying life in the last tight room.

Trudy Drucker
124

At Night

The blinds spin carlights in a moment's lace
To ravel shadow on my ceiling screen
And dapple black cat's back where he lies deep
In some contenting dream of cream or chase.
By some sense stirred, he wakens, blinking green,
And yawns his tongue around the taste of sleep.

Twilight Time

I like to swim late in the day, after the toddlers have been hustled home to supper and the teenagers have taken their blasters to more exciting places. That is when I have the pool in our River Vale, New Jersey, development to myself. These days, the pool has special value for me because I know it will soon be closed for the season.

When I'm tired of thrashing around, I turn on my back, float, watch and think. It's late, but not very late, in the day as well as the year. It will be hours before real night, weeks before winter's cold. I am 62, healthy, retired and with some good work still undone. I notice the confluence of my personal time with the time of the day and the year—an attractive metaphor but hardly perfect. The day and the year will renew themselves, but we get only one human winter each, and I have no hope that something like Christmas will occur in its deep middle. I don't fear the dark or hate the cold.

I float and watch the sky turn pewter. The new wind will ruffle my skin a bit when I get out of the water. So, not much longer now. Night. Winter. Old age. Time to get dry, to get warm, to get ready.

The Fifth Voyage

(From the diary of Mrs. Gulliver)

Lem's home again: this time, I think, for good;
I've brushed his clothes where they were pricked with hay.
I mind my temper, but I wish he would
Stop teaching our poor children how to neigh.

He put twelve feet between us at the table,
Refused good meat, and called for grain and oats.
He spends all morning chuckling in the stable;
The roan's in foal: Lord, how the old fool dotes.

Once I'd been proud to be a surgeon's wife,
To aid his every wish, and envy none.
He could have earned our living with his knife,
But he would sail, and what he willed, was done.

Oft was he shipwrecked (so he says) and I
Played Desdemona to the silly tales he'd spin
Of midgets, giants, islands in the sky—
On those long trips, they drink a lot of gin.

This last trip was the worst; such trials he braved,
Such hungers and such thirsts, so long off course.
With all my soul, I do thank God he's saved;
But God, where will we put another horse?

Last night, at last, he wished again to share
My long-cold bed, and vowed he'd love no other.
He said I smelled no worse than his worst mare.
Now, that's enough. I'm going home to Mother.

Trudy Drucker
128

Curtis Robbins

Curtis Robbins was born in New York City in 1943. He became deaf at the age of one from a near-fatal dose of a mycin drug he was given to treat tonsillitis. He received a B.A. from Gallaudet University in 1967, an M.A. from New York University in 1972, and a Ph.D. from the University of Maryland in 1985. He has been a vocational rehabilitation counselor, career counselor, sign language teacher, Jewish history teacher, computer programmer, and an assistant professor of educational technology. Robbins began writing poetry at the age of fourteen. His first published poem appeared in an NYU Deafness Center publication in 1971. His poems have been published in several Jewish newspapers and *The Second Jewish Catalog*, and several poems will be featured in two forthcoming anthologies. Curtis Robbins lives in College Park, Maryland, with his wife and two children.

Piano

It is vain for the singer to burst into clamour
With the great black piano appassionato. The glamour
Of childish days is upon me, my manhood is cast
Down in the flood of remembrance, I weep like a child for
    the past.

                D. H. Lawrence, "Piano"

How I've longed to play
          a sensible tune
                on a piano.

The piano —
      the piano intrigues me.

The long rows of white and black keys —
    an endless paradigm —
          no octave mattered,
   whether a bass semitone
            that vibed
        from the rightmost key
           or
        a trebling silence
        from the leftmost
            that felt like
      the felt hammer dropped.

How troubling!
        How droll!
Nothing makes any sense —
        this mystical piano.
Its presence radiates
      a certain splendor, though.

If only I had
    this magical touch,
        I'd finger a tune.

        How I've longed
         to play
        a sensible tune.

Curtis Robbins
130

The Big Black Beetle

The big black beetle —
he crossed the living room floor
while I was reading an anthology
of poems this sleepless night.

He scuttled quite promptly
to escape the uninviting light,
dimly radiant, this sleepless night.

His presence was a nuisance.
I was disturbed! All the stillness
of the living room, and the quiet
that surmises any night
was disrupted by his crawling
scramble, distracting my reading
this sleepless night.

This damned big black beetle. Why,
I had to slam my book shut,
throw it flatly and quickly—
putting an end to this sleepless night.

Homeless

The hot,
    humid, and
        humiliating
          summer
            heat.

       High sun mid-day.

Passing the worst part of today
      through
    the worse part of DC,
passing by a parochial school
         shut down for the summer.

    Parishioner kids are out on a
      drug-ridden, bullet-bitten
        street —
          running through
          a bleeding
            hydrant.

    A homeless man —
          his shopping cart
        of disheveled belongings
           parked
      at the wrought-iron gate
        sought refuge —
    naps
on the deserted
schoolfront
  stoop.

Curtis Robbins
132

Mary Holmes

Mary Holmes has a B.A. in English from Hood College and an M.A. in Dance from George Washington University. After many years of teaching and choreographing modern dance at the college level, she retired to concentrate on writing fiction and raising her two sons. "Inner Ears" is based on Holmes' experience. Her nerve deafness, which was caused by high doses of antibiotics in the early 1950s, is nearly total and is accompanied by severe tinnitus. Holmes is currently writing a novel.

Inner Ears

Bedtime is long past, but this is no time for sleeping. Quietly, I raise the window shade so I can peer through the limbs of the pin oak at the night sky. Settled back upon soft, flannel-cased pillows, I am ready to work on the Miss Warlow problem.

I am frightened still as I recall Miss Warlow slapping her half-specs on her desk, then walking to the door, face pulled up in a frown. I can never decide whether she is uglier with or without her glasses. Frizzy orange hair sticks out from brown roots on her head; although she is our school nurse, she resembles a witch, and the students at Resurrection School suspect she really is one. We are supposed to set a good example for her and pray for her conversion to Catholicism, but I know better: her soul is a lost cause. Shivering as I squirm in the cold metal chair, I wait for her to speak. Why don't the nuns allow us to wear sweaters, anyway?

She turns sharply. "I can't understand! Your first and second grade test scores were perfect, yet today's is quite poor. Can you explain?"

Perhaps. But not to you.

"Look, Miss Warlow, I hear fine! I'm doing okay in school. I even take piano lessons."

"Hmmmm. I have other pupils to screen now, so you may return to your room. I'm going to call you back, though, and I warn you: If you can't do better next time, I'll contact your parents. Good afternoon, Katherine."

My brown oxfords clunk as I race down the hallway to the girls' room. Sitting on the toilet with legs dangling, I drop my head into my hands. I could run away, just charge out the school door, but lacking that kind of bravery, I shuffle back to the classroom.

Sister Leo Rosaire's sweet voice welcomes me. "Come in, come in! I'm reading the class a Freddy the Pig book called *Wiggins for President.* We've just begun chapter one."

Freddy books are my favorites, and as the pretty young nun describes Jinx the cat and the animals in Mr. Bean's barnyard, calmness returns. Leaning with an elbow on my desk, I look at the rows of boys and girls and feel warmed. The sunny windows through which travel many fine daydreams, the smell of shavings around the pencil sharpener, the long row of library books next to the statue of the gentle Infant of Prague, the bulletin board decorated with leaves and our best compositions, all are precious parts of a place where I belong. No one, not even Miss Warlow, can disturb me here.

Yet, the next day, and six times more, she summons me for testing. The results are always the same: in the upper tones, substantial loss. Our studies of the lives of the saints have introduced us to a variety of tortures. I think about torment as I fail to hear the nurse on the other side of the Beltone machine.

The night grows darker, and I slide down between the sheets to watch the moon struggling to peek out from behind the clouds. Now, Miss Warlow, I shall tell you plainly what you want to know.

You changed the set-up, nurse! The first year, you marched the whole class to the church hall, where we sat four to a card table. Then you gave your speech.

"Today we're going to check how our ears work, because we all know how important our hearing is to being good students. I'm going to dictate a series of numbers to you through earphones, first the right side, then the left, and you will write down exactly what you hear. My voice will grow softer and softer, so you must concentrate and listen very carefully."

You plunked the phones on each child, making us look as if we were all about to be executed. Then you disappeared behind a screen. A few shocks of crackling noises made me think you were frying bacon, but suddenly you were speaking directly into our heads.

"Now we'll begin. Right ear. Nine-three."

Cinchy! I wrote 93.

"Five-eight."

Easy. 58

"One eight."

Not so clear, but searching through my memory of sounds, I landed upon short u, long a, and marked down 18.

"ii-ah."

A blur. What now? My eyes shot automatically across the table to Sammy Kirtland's paper, where I could see on his paper, 19. On my sheet, I penciled 61.

In the end, my columns of numbers were identical to Sammy's and all correct. Don't you see, Miss Warlow? This is what you do if you don't hear: you use your eyes! The funny thing is that you gave the numbers very slowly, making it easy for me to keep up. In second grade, I followed the same routine again, with outstanding results. But this year, your fancy new audiometer spoiled the game by testing us individually.

You don't seem to understand, Miss Warlow; my hearing is my private business. Like tooth-brushing, I take care of this myself. If I miss a word, the rest of the sentence supplies the idea. A speaker's mouth draws shapes of sounds, and any moron can tell by watching a person move whether he's angry, tired, or in a hurry. When friends laugh, I join in; you don't have to hear the punch line to enjoy it. I cheat, lie, guess, bluff, and piece clues together.

You haven't even asked if I have ringing in my ears. I do, but don't bother imagining Santa's sleighbells. Try tea kettles, ten at a time, hollering to be removed from a hot stove. Or close your eyes and listen to the fire company whizzing through your brain, sirens screeching. These horrid sounds were a mystery to me when I first noticed them, about four years ago, until I remembered one of my father's breakfast demonstrations.

He placed an orange on the table. "That's the sun!" he said. "Now this," he continued, reaching for a plum, "is the earth." Slowly, he turned the plum in small concentric circles, while tracing a large circle around the orange. "See? The earth rotates around the sun while it turns on its own axis!"

"No, no, Daddy," I laughed. "With all the spinning going on, how come we're not dizzy all the time?"

"Because the motion is verrry slow. Now then," he chirped, "we can call this banana the moon, and watch it tag alongside the earth." Under his fingertips, banana followed plum.

"I don't believe you, Dad!"

"Ah, but this is just the beginning, only a small portion of our solar system! There are others!" He grabbed the salt shaker and enthusiastically sprinkled granules around the edge of the table. "All the white specks are stars, and every one is a sun," he said with a flourish.

I laughed then, but the theory began to make sense when the noises started up. I figured that such tremendous movement in space must create sounds that everyone receives deep inside the ear. I'm a third-grader now, Miss Warlow; I realize I was wrong. The noises are mine alone, and you have no right knowing about them.

If only you could have met my Great-Aunt Lettie. She was a spinster, an old bag of an invalid, although I don't believe she was crippled. She wore a box hearing aid, half the size of her chest, with the battery turned off. My grown-up relatives snickered that she tuned out to save money, but once she told me otherwise. Whispering, as if to unbury some horror just for me, she explained that the sounds of her undergarments brushing against the microphone were a torture. "All that scritch-scritch-scritching shoots right through your earpiece, and drives you *crazy!*" she hissed. I hadn't really wanted to know, and I vowed that I would never enter Aunt Lettie's silent, musty, lonely world.

Rain clouds blot out the moon and sleep overtakes me. I

wake the next morning hoping Miss Warlow has died during the night, but as soon as I reach the school yard, I see her. During catechism, I am called to her office, but when I enter, the Beltone is nowhere in sight. Miss Warlow, minus her glasses, is not behind her desk, but sitting on the gray leather chaise in the corner, and she is actually smiling.

"Good morning, Kate! May I call you Kate? Sit right here by me, and we'll chat." Her speech is slow, with exaggerated enunciation, as though she is talking to a deaf person, but the tone of her voice is kind. "We must face your hearing problem, Kate; we can do it together. Your parents must be informed. Why haven't you told them yourself?"

"I dunno."

"But your mother and father will understand."

Understand what? That I'm different from everyone? That no kid in the third grade will want to be my friend?

"There's no need for them to know," I muttered stubbornly.

"Oh Kate. I do want to help you." She reaches out and pats my hand, her scratchy, overwashed skin causing me to shudder. She stares at me for some seconds, then releases my hand with a sigh and walks over to the desk, where she flips on the half-specs.

"In addition to your parents, I am obligated by law to report to the State Board of Health."

Great. They arrest kids for flunking hearing tests? You think this is Russia or something? "Please, Miss Warlow, don't do this!"

"I must, Katherine, whether I want to or not. You'll be fine, I promise. Go back to Sister Leo now, and try not to worry!"

Rising, but only barely, I leave the nurse's office as though breathing ether and wander through the halls until I find myself, by chance, in front of my classroom. Standing unnoticed, my forehead pressed to the door, I stare at the horizontal grain in the varnished oak and listen to the sirens in my ears rise in pitch and crescendo. My eyelids close tightly upon a picture of a knife stripping an apple, cutting around, from skin to core. The mangled fruit disappears when I open my eyes, but the sounds remain. Slowly, my weight shifts back toward my heels, the familiar brass knob turns in my hand, and I push open the door.

Edna Shipley-Conner

❖❖

Edna Shipley-Conner is the Deafened Adult Coordinator for the Deaf Counseling, Advocacy, and Referral Agency (DCARA) in Northern California. She is responsible for developing the services and programs for hard of hearing and deafened adults at DCARA. Shipley-Conner holds a B.A. in English and is currently a master's degree candidate in counseling with an emphasis in life transitions. She was co-editor of a two-volume anthology of women's poetry, *Women Talking, Women Listening*. She became severely hearing impaired during her midthirties.

On My Impending Deafness

When I consider hearing
Is the last sense lost before death,
And know that I've been dying
Since soon after my first breath,

Impatient, my soul seeks sound,
Not for God's need
But to store experiences not found
Written, thunder being lightning's deed.

How best the yoke of silence
Can my spirit bear?
What work to do while waiting?
What talents left to share.

Meanwhile, I'll use my hands like lightning
And transform the silence borne,
Into signs with new meaning, brightening
the darkness of fear into a new form

Milton, like you, I will not wait and stand,
But create a new world with mind and hand.

Edna Shipley-Conner
141

The Search

Bred in a Country where tradition
Was gospel sung with feeling
I was always off key.
Leaving behind the ninety and nine
Sifting grain in many fields
Sowing some of my own,
Finding new truths
As old as the Greeks
Seeking a tune I can sing
In Harmony with
The song of myself.

Oklahoma

From the plane window
I see clay red fields
Cut by plows
And connected by fence row stitches.
Streams and ponds fill
With brick-colored water.

This land called
The home of the Redman,
Sent here on the tearful trail
From their homes to the east,
Seems to have collected the blood
Shed from their feet on that long trip
Seeped into the soil,
Which rains nor dust can destroy,
And made it fertile.

In the spring
Redbuds bloom along creek beds,
In back yards and around the Capitol,
Trying to heal history
And free faith in the future.

Edna Shipley-Conner

David Wright

David Wright is perhaps the best known deaf poet in the world. Born in South Africa, he lost his hearing due to illness at the age of seven. Wright was educated in hearing schools and attended university in England. Wright is widely known as an editor of English fiction and poetry as well as a poet in his own right. His autobiography *Deafness* chronicles his experiences as a deaf man living in a hearing culture.

By the Effigy of St. Cecilia

Having peculiar reverence for this creature
Of the numinous imagination, I am come
To visit her church and stand before the altar
Where her image, hewn in pathetic stone,
Exhibits the handiwork of her executioner.

There are the axemarks. Outside, in the courtyard,
In shabby habit, an Italian nun
Came up and spoke: I had to answer, "Sordo."
She said she was a teacher of deaf children
And had experience of my disorder.

And I have had experience of her order
Interpenetrating chords and marshalled sound;
Often I loved to listen to the organ's
Harmonious and concordant interpretation
Of what is due from us to the creation.

But it was taken from me in my childhood
And those graduated pipes turned into stone.
Now, having travelled a long way through silence,
Within the church in Trastevere I stand
A pilgrim to the patron saint of music

And am abashed by the presence of this nun
Beside the embodiment of that legendary
Virgin whose music and whose martyrdom
Is special to this place: by her reality.
She is a reminder of practical kindness,

The care it takes to draw speech from the dumb
Or pierce with sense the carapace of deafness;
And so, of the plain humility of the ethos
That constructed, also this elaborate room
To pray for bread in; they are not contradictory.

David Wright
145

Monologue of a Deaf Man

Et lui comprit trop bien, n'ayant pas entendu.
                    Tristan Corbière

It is a good plan, and began with childhood
As my fortune discovered, only to hear
How much it is necessary to have said.
Oh silence, independent of a stopped ear,
You observe birds, flying, sing with wings instead.

Then do you console yourself? You are consoled
If you are, as all are. So easy a youth
Still unconcerned with the concern of a world
Where, masked and legible, a moment of truth
Manifests what, gagged, a tongue should have told;

Still observer of vanity and courage
And of these mirror as well; that is something
More than a sound of violin to assuage
What the human being most dies of: boredom
Which makes hedgebirds clamour in their blackthorn cage.

But did the brushless fox die of eloquence?
No, but talked himself, it seems, into a tale.
The injury, dominated, is an asset;
It is there for domination, that is all.
Else what must faith do deserted by mountains?

David Wright
146

Talk to me then, you who have so much to say,
Spectator of the human conversation,
Reader of tongues, examiner of the eye,
And detective of clues in every action,
What could a voice, if you heard it, signify?

The tone speaks less than a twitch and a grimace.
People make to depart, do not say "Goodbye."
Decision, indecision, drawn on every face
As if they spoke. But what do they really say?
You are not spared, either, the banalities.

In whatever condition, whole, blind, dumb,
One-legged or leprous, the human being is,
I affirm the human condition is the same,
The heart half broken in ashes and in lies,
But sustained by the immensity of the divine.

Thus I too must praise out of a quiet ear
The great creation to which I owe I am
My grief and my love. O hear me if I cry
Among the din of birds deaf to their acclaim
Involved like them in the not unhearing air.

David Wright
147

Selections from Deafness

It is quite natural. Some hear more pleasantly with the eyes than with the ears. I do.

Gertrude Stein

About deafness I know everything and nothing. Everything, if forty years' firsthand experience is to count. Nothing, when I realize the little I have had to do with the converse aspects of deafness—the other half of the dialogue. Of that side my wife knows more than I. So do teachers of the deaf and those who work among them; not least, people involuntarily but intensely involved—ordinary men and women who find themselves, from one cause or another, parents of a deaf child. For it is the non-deaf who absorb a large part of the impact of the disability. The limitations imposed by deafness are often less noticed by its victims than by those with whom they have to do.

Deafness is a disability without pathos. Dr. Johnson called it "the most desperate of human calamities." Yet its effects are slapstick:

"Where's the baby?"

"I put it in the dustbin."*

There is a buffoonery about deafness which is liable to rub off on anybody who comes into contact with it. Having to shout at the hard of hearing is not elegant, nor is finger-spelling or the mouthing of words to magnify lip movement for those whose eyes are their ears. Deafness is a banana skin: an aspect which may conveniently be illustrated by an anec-dote I recently came across in an old memoir. It concerns the once famous but now forgotten Victorian poet, Alexander Smith. Variations of this incident, I may add, have pursued me through life. Smith, then a young man in the early bloom of literary repute, had been taken by Swinburne's friend John

* To a lipreader the words *baby* and *paper* are indistinguishable.

Nichol to pay his respects to that formidable but deaf blue-stocking, Harriet Martineau:

> Miss Martineau, it is otherwise well known, is a little hard of hearing. When the travellers arrived, several ladies were with her, and by the little circle of petticoats they were received with some *empressment*. Mr. Nichol took up the running, and some little conversation proceeded, Smith, in the racing phrase, *waiting*. Presently he "came with a rush" and observed it "had been a very fine day"—an unimpeachable and excellent remark which brought him instantly into difficulties. Miss Martineau was at once on the *qui vive*. The poet had made a remark probably instinct with fine genius, worthy of the author of *The Life Drama*. "Would Mr. Smith be so good as to repeat what he said?" Mr. Smith—looking, no doubt, uncommonly like an ass—repeated it in a somewhat higher key. Alas! Alas! in vain. The old lady shook her head. "It was really *so* annoying, but she did not quite catch; would Mr. Smith be *again* so good?" and her hand was at her eager ear. The unhappy bard, feeling, as he said, in his distress as if suicide might be the thing, shrieked and again shrieked his little piece of information—symptoms of ill-suppressed merriment becoming obvious around him. Finally the old lady's ear-trumpet was produced, and proceeding to shriek through this instrument, of which the delicate use was unknown to him, the bard nearly blew her head off.

The suffering, it will be seen, lay more to the side of Mr. Smith than the deaf lady, even if she did nearly have her head blown off. Hard to bear is the devaluation of whatever one may be saying—which is almost inevitable after its fourth or fifth repetition. Yet the anecdote illustrates an undramatic but not minor disadvantage of deafness, felt less positively by the deaf than their hearing friends: having to dispense with the easy exchange of trivialities which is oil to the wheels of conversation and to the business of living. The use of language as gesture, as reassuring noise rather than an instrument of specific communication, is largely denied the deaf.

Harriet Martineau, who underwent a partial loss of hearing at the age of twenty, was one of the relatively few to write about deafness from experience. There is a surprising amount of unsentimental good sense in the *Letter to the Deaf,* bossy and dogmatic though she is. However, she does put her finger on a main problem of describing deafness at first hand, when she recognizes how far the experience of it must vary from one person to another. That it must differ according to the severity of the hearing loss is obvious.

Very few are absolutely deaf. Their experience must necessarily be different from that of the severely deaf, the partially deaf, and the merely hard of hearing. The partially deaf, it seems to me, have the worst of both worlds. They hear enough to be distracted by noise yet not enough for it to be meaningful. For the merely hard of hearing there is the strain of extracting significance from sounds that may be as loud as life yet out of focus; what comes through is an auditory fuzz. Of course there are hearing-aids, but not everybody can profit from these . . . .

It is as a deaf person that I write this book, though deafness does not seem to me to be a disproportionate element of the predicament in which I find myself; that is to say the predicament in which we are all involved because we live and breathe. If vocation means anything, I suppose myself a poet. Whether I am that is disputable, but the deafness remains a fact.

· · · · · · ·

Now I must emphasize that I am completely without hearing—a fact, so rum is the operation of human vanity, on which I rather pique myself. (When introducing me to people my mother still says, "He's a little deaf"—a euphemism I find vaguely defamatory.) Total deafness is comparatively rare, which may be an advantage from the point of view of this book—such a degree of deafness may serve as a criterion.

I do not live in a world of complete silence. There is no such thing as absolute deafness. Coming from one whose aural nerve is extinct, this statement may be taken as authoritative.

Let me attempt to define the auditory limits of the world I inhabit. They are perhaps less restricted than may be imagined . . . If I stand on a wooden floor I can "hear" footsteps behind me, but not when standing on a floor made of some less resonant substance—for example stone or concrete. I can even partially "hear" my own voice . . . Yet like nearly all deaf people I cannot judge the loudness or quality of my own voice. To some extent I can do so by putting a finger against my Adam's apple or voicebox . . . . Likewise, I "hear" a piano if I place a finger on it while it is being played; a radio and gramophone too, when touching the sound box or amplifier . . . Such "hearing" is selective; I receive only the low notes of the scale, the high ones elude me. No matter how loud the volume is turned on, what comes through is a bent or incomplete version of actual sound. In "touch-hearing" most music, and all speech, comes across as a blurry bumble of noise.

Nevertheless, there is some music that I enjoy after a fashion. But it has to be produced by stringed instruments (harp, guitar, piano, double-bass, and so on) as I cannot hear wind-instruments (flute, bagpipes, oboe). Percussive instruments like drums are naturally well inside my range. I have a passion for military bands, though hearing little except the drumtaps, a sad boom-thud from the big drum and a clattering exhilaration from the kettledrums. But I can't recognize a tune, not even "God Save the Queen." Since I lost my hearing there is only one musical work of which I can lay my hand on my heart and say it has truly given me an aesthetic experience. This is Bach's *Italian* Concerto. When I was an undergraduate at

Oxford a German friend of mind often played it on the piano. The piece bewitched me. Luckily it was one of his favourites for I used to make him play the concerto over and over again. Perhaps rather highbrow a bit of music to get a fixation on. Yet when he tried me out with Beethoven, Mozart, Mendelssohn, and even other pieces by Bach, I got nothing. Later I "listened" to Sibelius, Britten, Stravinsky and so forth— to all sorts of music, folk, pop, and concrete—but none of them meant a thing.

Though it is nearly a quarter of a century since I heard it played, the *Italian* Concerto remains part of my spiritual furniture. Not long ago I tried to reproduce what I could remember of it, or rather of its effect upon myself, in the course of a poem. I offer the verses here for their interest as attempted onomatopoeic recreation of piano music as heard, so to speak, by deaf ears:

Piano

Openhanded, opionated, cracked, she lived alone
Survivor of ordinary sorrows: which to assuage
Death, being no enemy, subtracted her from knowledge.
She is now and forever absent from her music-room
Unless as an essence contained in its weatherwarped thin
Panellings impregnated with the repeated passage
And phrasing of Beethoven, Brahms. Their reverberate message
She would draw from a grand piano, plundering from the strung

Harp hidden within, cunningly manipulating
The obedience of keys as some Dresden musician taught her—
Flood and ebb of sonata over an empty lawn
Clear of a ratiocination of grief—rapt in her
Artificial beatitude, world constucted of sound,
The articulate mathematical order of which we are given an
    inkling.

David Wright
152

To get on with the list of things audible, or at least interfering with the silence that might be expected to compensate a totally occluded ear, let me tabulate the following: gunfire, detonation of high-explosive, low-flying aeroplanes, cars backfiring, motor-bicycles, heavy lorries, carts clattering over cobblestones, wurlitzers, pneumatic drills. There can't be much that I miss of the normal orchestration of urban existence. I should add that I also, once, heard the human voice. One day in 1963 I was at Lord's cricket ground; Ted Dexter had just come in to bat against the West Indies. He put a couple of runs on the board with the air of a man who means to get another ninety-eight before lunch. Suddenly he was bowled. While the bails were still flying, coats, hats, cushions, umbrellas, sandwiches, for all I know babies even, were hurled into the air by some nine or ten thousand West Indians in the free seats where I was watching. Up went a simultaneous roar of delight. Hearing that sound, for me not very loud but like a croaking bark, was a queer and spooky experience. I have never forgotten it.

It will be seen that the world a deaf man inhabits is not one of complete silence, which is perhaps the chief complaint he has to make about it. There is another point. Though noise, as such, does not obtrude to the extent that the above catalogue would seem to imply, the world in which I live seldom *appears* silent. Let me try to explain what I mean. In my case, silence is not absence of sound but of movement.

Suppose it is a calm day, absolutely still, not a twig or leaf stirring. To me it will seem quiet as a tomb though hedgerows are full of noisy but invisible birds. Then comes a breath of air, enough to unsettle a leaf; I will see and hear that movement like an exclamation. The illusory soundlessness has been interrupted. I see, as if I heard, a visionary noise of wind in a disturbance of foliage. Wordsworth in a late poem exactly caught the phenomenon in a remarkable line:

A soft eye-music of slow-waving boughs

which may have subconsciously derived from an equally
cogent line in Coleridge's *The Eolian Harp:*

A light in sound, a sound-like power of light.

The "sound" seen by me is not necessarily equivalent to the
real one. It must often be close enough, in my case helped by
a subliminal memory of things once heard. I cannot watch a
gale without "hearing" an uproar of violent movement: trees
thrashing, grassblades battling and flattened; or, at sea, waves
locked and staggering like all-in wrestlers—this kind of thing
comes through as hubbub enough. On the other hand I also
live in a world of sounds which are, as I know quite well,
imaginary because nonexistent. Yet for me they are part of
reality. I have sometimes to make a deliberate effort to
remember I am not "hearing" anything, because there is nothing to hear. Such nonsounds include the flight and movement
of birds, even fish swimming in clear water or the tank of an
aquarium. I take it that the flight of most birds, at least at a
distance, must be silent—bar the creaking noise made by the
wings of swans and some kinds of wild geese. Yet it *appears*
audible, each species creating a different "eye-music," from
the nonchalant melancholy of seagulls to the staccato flitting
of tits.

This is not to subscribe to the irritating theory that the loss
of one sense is compensated for by the quickening of another.
There are no compensations, life is not like that. At best we
are offered alternatives. We have no choice but to take them.

This is by no means a complete picture of the world I live
in, or of any other deaf person's, come to that. Almost nothing
has been said about the major hurdle of deafness, the problem
of communication. It is simply an attempt to convey what
deafness is like physically, or at least what it's like so far as

one deaf man is concerned, before I go on to tell the story of how I lost my hearing, how I reacted, how I was educated, and the various stratagems necessity forced me to adopt to get on and get by in a non-deaf world.

For I am now, after forty years of what we will term silence, so accommodated to it (like a hermit-crab to its shell) that were the faculty of hearing restored to me tomorrow it would appear an affliction rather than a benefit. I do not mean that I find deafness desirable but that in the course of time the disability has been assimilated to the extent that it is now an integral condition of existence, like the use of a hand. By the same token the restoration of my hearing, or the loss of my deafness, whichever is the right way of putting it, would be like having that hand cut off.

So it was in dead of winter, on a tenebrous afternoon, I arrived at Northampton. It was my fourteenth birthday. Term was nearly half done; I had missed its first weeks because of our inadvertent stopover at Mombasa.

The taxi from the station had taken us through the centre of the town, past soon-to-be-familiar All Saints' with its statue of Charles II in Roman toga and peruke, a Victorian town hall and dun-coloured general hospital. The school turned out to be a solid, nineteenth-century stuccoed brick mansion with a pillared portico standing in what, before the speculative deposits of the early thirties, had been an outer suburb of Northampton. The house hid behind tall hedges of thick yew and holly.

A maid in cap and apron, white face slashed with a purple hare-lip, answered the bell. My mother and I were shown into a cluttered, pleasantly chintzy, firelit sitting-room, where the principal and his wife awaited us. Yet I remember nothing of this first encounter with that extraordinary Welshman of the gold monocle, Augustan features, prescriptive will, implacable charm, obssesive patience and fiery choler. All impressions were blotted out by my introduction, half an hour later, to that other world to which I belonged but was yet to enter.

This new life began as soon as I had said good-bye to my mother. I was ushered along a dark cupboardy passage that led to the dining-room. It was late afternoon, or early evening. The senior boys were at supper, the one meal of the day not presided over by any member of the staff. This accident plunged me *in medias res* among my future companions, uninhibited by the presence of authority or of outsiders from the hearing world. Up till then I had had no contact to speak of with the deaf. This was my initiation to their freemasonry. I went in at the deep end.

A long table at the back of the dining-room seats perhaps a dozen boys. Is the verb right? Confusion stuns the eye, arms whirl like windmills in a hurricane, thunderous unbroken drumming assaults what's left of the ear. Heelthuds shake the floor while someone hammers on the table. Mouths frame words: vowels and consonants blown up like photographic enlargements, every syllable reinforced by the emphatic silent vocabulary of the body—look, expression, bearing, glance of eye; hands perform their pantomime. Absolute engrossing pandemonium. Nothing I was ever to come across in later life held a candle to this scene—not even the saloon bars and late-night cafes of Soho and Fitzrovia in the forties. Yet this is a normal supper (at other meals, under the eye of the staff, behaviour is circumscribed) such as I am to participate in every evening for the next five years, and never turn a hair.

I begin to sort out what's going on. The seemingly corybantic brandishing of hands and arms reduces itself to a convention, a code which as yet conveys nothing. It is in fact a kind of vernacular. The school has evolved its own peculiar language or argot, though not a verbal one.

Tableau: an argument is going on. Two boys try to impress

their points of view on a third, who won't listen but defends his opinion by keeping downturned eyes fixed upon his plate. Did he glance up he might read the words they were saying and be lost. The other two, one on each side, hammer their knuckles against either shoulder to make him look up. Realizing he won't, one of them grabs his head, wrenches it round till the eyes are level with his mouth. This idea is taken up by the other, who now seizes the head and jerks it back again to point at his own face. Owner of head bears the man-handling with perfect indifference and perfect determination not to be communicated with. He has screwed his eyes tight shut.

Around this contretemps the meal proceeds. At supper everyone is allowed to bring his own provender, which may be anything from sardines to cocoa, pickled onions, cake, cornflakes, tinned pineapple, jam, dates, God knows what. While apparently engaging every limb and feature in the ser-vice of communication, all simultaneously prepare and dis-patch the food in front of them, offering one another fruit and cake and biscuits, slopping milk and sugar over bowls of cere-al. It's like watching a three-ring circus.

This has taken time to describe, but in fact I am not given more than a moment to absorb the spectacle before being— well, not introduced, but sucked into the irresistible maelstrom of energy pulsating round the supper-table. Remarks are shot at and about me, eatables pressed hospitably into my hands.

To reproduce their talk by transcribing no more than the words actually used must misrepresent and distort its quality. Its life and subtlety (the observation and humour were often subtle) depended on expressive demeanour, face, and eye, on mimic gift: the pantomimic gesture subsuming a cartoonist's graphic ability to seize, magnify, and focus some essential point. The words constitute perhaps twenty per cent of the means of communication; their job seems mainly to specify or pinpoint what's being discussed. Gesture and expression then take over, to elaborate and qualify. A framework of spoken nouns is enough—mime does the work of a verb, a grimace offers the adjective. On the basis of one uttered vocable may be erected whole sentences and paragraphs.

But for the record I set down the words as spoken, running together in a single paragraph the contributions of half-a-dozen speakers, the remarks made to or at me, as they came:

"John Wright. From South Africa. Brown! Brown! Look brown! Hot! Look! BRRROWN! (They were admiring my African suntan, which must have looked rather conspicuous in February.) Sun! Whew! Do you like girls? Shut up! I'm tired of you! I'm talking! Plymouth, me. Jimmy Boyce is South African. Jimmy! Jimmy! Shut up! Listen to me! I'm talking to John Wright. Jimmy Boyce is Johannesburg! Do you like England? Rain, rain, wet, cold, dark, sad, sad, no fruit. This is William. He is very poor. This is Julian Watson. He is Head Prefect. Jimmy has a girl friend. True! True! This is Henry Garnet. He is mad. Mad. Yes you are. MAD. Shut up! Wrong, wrong! Thought. You THOUGHT! Have you seen the king? I saw the king. This is Dermot. Clever. Brains, brains. Dermot has a letter from the king. Mad! Mad! Not the king. Buckingham Palace. I saw! I saw! Shut up! Be quiet! I'm tired of you! Do you like swimming? We swim in summer. Down there at Midsummer Meadow. Girls not allowed. Very sad. Very SA-A-AD! Very MEL-ANCH-O-LY!"

The last speaker would have been Charles Oakley, a boy of doleful countenance, given to the collection of polysyllabic vocables and extraordinary epithets, most of which he picked up in the Shakespeare class. (I remember one day, when I had annoyed him, he turned upon me and remarked with lugubrious deliberation: "Hag-seed!")

The deaf-and-dumb alphabet we never used; it was strictly against the rules of the school. Most of the pupils, like myself, had never even learnt it. All communications were supposed to be oral. Our own sign-argot was of course prohibited, like another habit we had of not using the voice when forming words (it makes for easier lipreading apart from the obvious advantage of cutting the risk of being overheard). But these rules could not be enforced without the presence of the staff. What I have been describing is not how we talked, but how we talked among ourselves when no hearing person was present. At such time our behaviour and conversation were quite different. We relaxed inhibitions, wore no masks. But the presence of the hearing naturally constrained our modes of communication. Besides, in front of hearing people we would try to appear "normal."

Cynthia Amerman

Cynthia Amerman has taught Spanish at Sussex County Community College and English, Spanish, and Creative Writing at Hilltop Country Day School in Sparta, New Jersey. After graduating from Allegheny College, she lived in Ecuador where she taught English at the Colegio Americano de Quito. She has studied writing at Columbia University, English Literature at Drew University, and is working on a literary translation project to complete an M.Litt. degree at Drew. Amerman is currently studying American Sign Language at Union County College and competing on the Berkeley Aquatic Club Masters swimming team. She lives in New Jersey at Blair Academy with her husand Peter, and children Evelyn Avery-Jones and Alexander Amerman.

Aeaea

Whichever way you spell it
Circe's island is made
of vowels, round sound
turning sorcerer's shapes on the tongue
as suckling breast milk
averts a crush of consonants,
                language

                AIAIA

cry of anguished birth
old pattern, song struck
like lightning
on each traveler
indelible, invisible
                burn

Cynthia Amerman
161

Game of Hide-and-Seek

i

under the infinite sky
we wander in the same garden
beneath the hedges of the labyrinth
we see only each other's feet

the warm trees
enclose us with their tender branches
the flowers
strike with their haunting fragrance
songs of longing
and with our parched lips
we speak only silence

ii

In the house of my grandparents
I saw my dead son
at the top of the stairs
he was watching
our game of hide and seek
I said to him: Do you want to come down?
He answered: No.

Cynthia Amerman
163

Woodville

I visit you
in this brick forest of barred windows
where you live your nightmares
They let me in

Georgia uses her skin for an ashtray
black skin with blacker polka dots
Behind a column a toothless puppet
dances his love dance,
drooling, pushing himself against the post
for the final act

Hey Beth! Remember us, green
jumpered elves playing Robin Hood
in the clearing?
Funny phone calls?
You telling me
what to say to David?
Sun streams through the bars and scatters
particles of outside come in
with me, in my hair, on my clothes
A betrayal

She laughs like a chain saw at nothing
funny, her puffy fingers kneading me:
Don't you hear that bluebird bitching?
And the crow? Followed me here from Boston
Oh Jesus! What part do I play? Leaves
from Cathay, I rhyme myself sane.

I press your shoulder, Beth!
A charm to break the spell
A kiss, hoping some magic
will wake you
from the deathly dreaming
I rush
down the dark arcade
to where the light thickens and
they let me out.

Cynthia Amerman
164

Birth

Look how quick and easy
it is what they do
with their bodies
stocking the lake with
millions of hopeful salmon
spawning
but only one will be
(the lone one)
survivor by oceanic union,
lake turned seaworld.
Look how slow, how complicated
it is what we do with our bodies
how the burgeoning water
churns, thrashes its
seaweed to and fro.
Cradles of flesh
we are/flashing forth
with foam and blood/
fish-pink being
fully formed
seedling turned
heartbeat,
looking amputation
in the eye
(the one as many).

Cynthia Amerman
165

Medusa

that look you use
masks a solid core
of sadness, legacy of your
mortality
punished for love
your serpent participation
glistens among us
your shining scales
your fierce teeth
bleed a raw beauty
that turns me to flesh
and I begin

Karin Mango

Karin Mango has been hearing impaired since her teens. Her first book, a novel, was published when she was fourteen. She has since published thirteen other books, including fiction and nonfiction for young adults, as well as many articles. She works part-time as the librarian at the New York League for the Hard of Hearing. Mango grew up in Reading, England, and received her M.A. from Edinburgh University, Scotland and her M.L.S. from Pratt Institute in New York. She and her husband live in Brooklyn, New York. They have two grown children, both married.

To Your Health

Now let me see: it says here ". . . powdered rhinoceros horne, an Amulet against Accidents . . . an Aphrodisiac . . ." mmm, interesting, but not the point just now. I carefully turned the page in the ancient leather-bound book. "Also, through the Animal's fine Hearing, said to be of Salutary Effect in Weaknesses of the Ear." Aha! The only problem might be how to obtain a rhinoceros horn, with or without the "e," since they are an endangered species. I'm not worried about the powdering: I have a Cuisinart.

What I'm doing is research. We all have an obligation to look after our health. When you have something without a "cure," like hearing impairment, once you have done all you can in other respects and it hasn't really helped, you can't just sit back and give up.

I have done all the other things. I have been to doctors. I have annual checkups. I look after my aids and other assistive devices.

I exercise. I admit to getting out of breath when I run for a bus, and I have doubts about mountain climbing as well as vertigo, but I can walk till the cows come home. I can also jump rope, even double-overs. Aerobic exercise: I'm even fashionable.

Food: I eat sensibly. No octopus, no sheep's eyes, no tripe, no haggis. Well, all right—I keep the cholesterol level down, I avoid refined sugar and flour, I cut down on the salt. I eat dark green and deep yellow things and all that. The ears are the most energy-hungry organs of the body. I feed them well. I don't smoke; I try to avoid caffeine. On the other hand, I'm happy to know that a glass of wine a day is actually good for you.

I've explored alternative therapies. I haven't had the courage yet to try hypnotherapy. What if I turn into the

Sphinx or develop a craving for toothpaste? But I have taken courses in biofeedback and acupuncture, and they helped. I'm a little more relaxed about things. And more assertive through assertiveness training.

Maybe the lifting of a certain amount of tension resulting from these courses gave me the idea of further research.

I started looking around. I had been taking calcium and fluoride because the doctor had told me that these, taken with vitamins including Vitamin D, might harden the bones in the inner ear, softened, like mine, by otospongiosis.

So, if calcium, why not zinc, too? I'd read that certain dietary deficiencies may make your hearing worse. Parts of the ear have a very high zinc content. Obviously I had a zinc deficiency. "Zinc" reminded me of old bathtubs and greasy ointment. I was glad to discover it also came in pill form. I wouldn't have to down a succession of bathtubs.

After giving it a fair try, I saw that there was no effect. The zinc joined the calcium and fluoride on the kitchen shelf.

I looked around some more. Lecithin. A combination of lecithin and cholesterol exists in many foods. When taken together, the lecithin dissolves the cholesterol. Without lecithin, cholesterol builds up in the arteries and may impair hearing by collecting in the blood vessels of the ear. I was horrified: I thought I'd been watching the cholesterol. Evidently not enough. I added a big container of lecithin granules to the collection in the kitchen.

Of course you need the right amount of vitamins and minerals to supplement your diet in order to be healthy. The simple vitamins that went with the calcium and fluoride weren't enough, I saw. I needed megavitamins.

After awhile a thought struck me. How did all these things know where to go? I couldn't put up a road sign: "TO THE EAR." For all I knew, everything was draining into my feet, those aerobic walkers. Or fighting like crazy all around my body. And even if they knew where to go, certainly nothing was improving up there in my ears.

I regained my common sense and cut down on the pills. But I continued my research. And now I had another shock. I learned that certain drugs may be harmful to hearing. I knew about the mycin group and I'd thought that was all. Now I saw a list as long as my arm—as were most of the names. I recognized some, though, and thought fast. What had I been using? Aspirin for that headache, iodine for the cut finger, camphor for the blankets. Even ordinary pencils have lead in them, for heaven's sake. And, unlike the vitamins and minerals that hadn't a clue, these things obviously knew exactly where they were heading. Straight for my ears.

I had at least learned something. Keep off, where possible, and read labels. The latter isn't a problem to me as I read everything including cereal boxes and matchbooks.

But I have not given up, even if I am reaching into rather esoteric areas. Maybe an amulet is all one needs. There must be one for hearing health. We have, after all, an obligation to look after our health.

I do know one thing. When I get old and am in need of home health care, I shall be impossible. I already pity the person who will try to help me. I shall be a know-it-all, far more knowledgeable than the trained professional. I'll have read everything, experimented with everything. I'll have had a cochlear implant. I shall eat only food grown at a little farm in northeast Iowa. I shall drink a glass of wine a day—a big one. I shall have tried and rejected every known assistive device and will have reverted to a cracked and favorite Victorian ear trumpet.

I shall have had hypnotherapy and will have turned into the Sphinx with a craving for toothpaste.

Christmas Cheer

Maybe the best idea would be to pack a small bag with books and Hershey bars and go away to an isolated cottage somewhere in the wilds. Peacefully alone over Christmas. It was tempting, even if I were accidentally to pack junk mail and Proust instead of James Michener and Agatha Christie.

No straining to hear above a hubbub of voices. No explaining: "I have a hearing loss—would you say that again, please? And again? Just one more time, in different words?" No resentment over yet again being the "odd man out" in a holiday group of chatting people. What good was "Hark, the Herald Angels Sing" when you couldn't hark to them yourself? And when all the family was gathered together so rarely and it was so important to hear them, not to understand two connected sentences. Christmas cheer? Not that way.

It wouldn't have to be anywhere exotic like Bermuda or the Bahamas. I'd even take New Jersey—a stone's throw from home in New York—if it was quiet.

The feeling started soon after Thanksgiving. "Panic" was too strong a word, and it wasn't depression. "Mixed feelings" was more like it. Very mixed. I love festivals and traditions, and Christmas has always been my favorite. But with my hearing loss creeping annually down the scale from mild to moderate to severe and now severe to profound, all the things I had loved—people, festivities, carol-singing, getting together— were being slowly and inexorably pulled from my resisting grasp. As I saw the signs of Christmas appearing all around, in store decorations, Christmas tree vendors with their "forests" at street corners, the first cards arriving . . . the sensation intensified in my mind—and in my stomach—as I thought, How will I manage with so little intelligible sound? I miss such a lot. It's not worth the effort. Why not just say, "See you after the New Year" and even leave my TT behind?

Karin Mango
171

I thought about it quite seriously. First, I would leave the festive food ready for my husband and for Nick and Helen when they arrived from out of town. Then, we simply wouldn't give a party that year. I wouldn't get angry and resentful at the various gatherings of the season. I wouldn't have to be frustrated by the carol service at the church—a small thing, but emblematic of the whole season. I wouldn't get so tired by the sheer effort to communicate that all I wanted was escape.

Escape from the thick glass wall behind which so many of us hearing impaired people live. On the other side we see the lips moving, the easy communication, the connections with our fellow men and women, the laughter, the conversation, the discussions. All the things we sweat to get a mere inkling of. Outsiders at the window, looking in.

If you allow yourself to look at it that way.

It can be very easy to get into that frame of mind. It does seem a solution to escape and be safely, quietly alone. But as I went on thinking, it was clear I had to look at it differently. Not "escape," because it wasn't that at all. What I might be starting was the easy, deadly path to withdrawal and isolation, losing the ground so carefully achieved through adapting to the hearing loss and learning to live with it as best I could.

And what I'd been thinking of certainly wouldn't do much for my family's Christmas spirit. Not a brave "escape," merely a self-centered, cowardly running away.

Now that I was no longer looking through a haze of anxiety, common sense started to reassert itself. I didn't have to hear everything or struggle beyond reason. People would help me. What I didn't hear, I wouldn't hear. It wasn't only words that were important.

I sat down with my husband, Tony, and we planned our party. "Let's make it an open house," he suggested. "People will come in smaller groups and that will mean less noise to try to hear through. Easier for everyone." It was easier already.

It was a good party, with neighbors from our brownstone area. Truthfully, I didn't hear much and, yes, I did read a lot. But it wasn't either junk mail or Agatha Christie. It was the conversations carried on in writing to supplement my hearing aids and keep my friends from going mad with repetition. I had also forgotten that they were friends, who knew about my hearing loss, knew how to help me and were willing to do so.

Before Christmas, my son Nick brought his girlfriend to dinner. She is thoughtful and patient and in the quiet of home we managed quite passably. Then my daughter Helen brought her new boyfriend for us to meet. I looked at the beard hopelessly. How would I ever lipread him? I wanted to be at least minimally intelligent and communicative with someone who's important to her.

"What can I do to make conversation easier?" He asked the perfect question.

"Shave off the beard!" was my sincere but unspoken wish. But that was not what he meant and anyway it looked good on him. Instead, I took him into good light, asked him to speak slowly, Helen helped, and we could—sort of—talk. And "sort of" didn't matter.

The carol service is on Christmas Eve. Poinsettias were on the altar, a huge Christmas tree beside it; candles filled the church with their gentle light. Over the past years I have been going for the family company and the beauty of the scene. Forget the service, forget the minister speaking, forget the carols.

Well, this year it was still forget the first two items (and now I thought, common sense uppermost at last, how about getting a loop installed?), but surely carols are meant to be sung! The music, distorted and cacophonous to my damaged ears, was still familiar inside my head. I sang along, inaudible to myself, but no heads turned. I went on singing happily.

Karin Mango
173

Christmas Day. We always take the festive lunch to a tetchy and touchy old aunt who never leaves her house. We all helped her celebrate in spite of herself, heading off her impatience with my hearing difficulties. She has her own problems of failing hearing and sight and arthritic legs. I have only one thing wrong with me.

But still, the next evening, invited to a gathering across the street from our house, with people overflowing the rooms, with the noise and effort and straining to catch a minimal something, I nearly despaired. I couldn't hear Tony's familiar voice trying to help me, no quiet place, no room for paper messages. I reminded myself firmly of a couple of things. Sometimes it's not defeat to withdraw, but common sense. You don't have to be a part of everything—and you can also be part in various ways. It isn't only words that matter; it's people. I rested my ears and relaxed.

On the day both Nick and Helen had to leave, we all sat around the kitchen table eating Christmas leftovers. I looked at the faces around me. I no longer wanted to be in New Jersey or wherever it was by myself. With gratitude, love, and a small but definite feeling of success, I raised my glass: "*Christmas cheers!*"

Eddie Swayze

❖

Eddie Swayze is a poet, artist, and performer who composes work in both American Sign Language and English. He has performed his poetry for the Deaf Poetry Conference and the Deaf Poetry Series at the National Technical Institute for the Deaf, at the Pyramid Arts Center Gallery, and at The Bristol Mountain Festival. Swayze grew up in upstate New York, where he attended the Total Communication Program, a special education program for deaf children, at Horseheads High School. After graduating in 1983, he went on to receive a Bachelor of Fine Arts degree in Painting and Illustration from Rochester Institute of Technology. Currently, he works as Exhibit Specialist for Deaf Artists of America Gallery, the only gallery run and owned by a deaf person, in Rochester, New York.

A Statue of Virgin Mary

(A portrait of Patti Smith by R. Mapplethorpe)

Your Brancusi oblong face
Radiate smooth snow-white.
Your black water fall hair
With silver threads glisten.
Your long thin neck
Is a base for your Brancusi's face.

You are a statue of Virgin Mary
Wearing a thick Robert Mapplethorpe leather jacket.
It's a shrine to remember forever.
The radiating white background behind you
Is Albino-White-Hair heaven for Andy Warhol's peace.
You look down as a compassionate Mary
Toward a life of birth;
Your little blue Jackson Smith.

Eddie Swayze

Emily Mandelbaum

Emily Mandelbaum is a home-maker who has also worked as a museum technician, income tax preparer, and consultant to initiate community composting. Born to Quaker teachers in rural upstate New York, Mandelbaum received a B.A. in political science from Oberlin College, and an M.S. in geology from New York University. She values simple living, conservation of resources, ecosystem preservation, minimal consumption, and peace. She is profoundly hard of hearing, with an inherited, sensorineural hearing loss.

Mandelbaum writes poetry as an outlet to feelings or to comment on and explore "ordinary images." These are her first published poems.

Skiing In January 1991

I saw blood on the snow
on Cascade ski slopes.

Urgent pits of deep red
broke my glide midslope,
lacerated the whiteness,
invaded billows of flakes
demanded answers.

Blood, stay where you belong
on city streets,
hospital emergency rooms,
highway accident scenes,
Central America,
sands of the Persian Gulf.

Stay off the pure white ski slopes
where lifts hum and gently vibrate,
and sway us high
to the quiet winter world

Leave us alone with evergreens
that keep the peace as we glide and weave
our way down,
then rise up again, and again.

Disappear beneath new fallen snow,
fresh crystals piled deep
that reflect all light,
Repel your pigments,
recoat our skiers world
with soft, unbroken whiteness.

Emily Mandelbaum
179

Sounds

What happened to the sounds
that once arrived so easily
and needed no analysis,
no technology,
no queries?

The interface was clear as glass,
no aural fog to penetrate,
no confusion to resolve,
no context to decipher.

Now sounds attack,
fire volleys of puzzles
that require visual clues,
frequency analysis,
amplifiers,
guesses,
reasoning,
quick solutions
before the next barrage.

Emily Mandelbaum
180

Jack Clemo

Jack Clemo was born in a village in Cornwall, where he continued to live until his death in 1977. Throughout his life, he suffered from recurrent losses of both vision and hearing and was, for much of his adult life, completely deaf-blind. Despite having ended his formal education at the age of thirteen, Clemo became a brilliant poet, known for his passionate verse and vivid descriptions of the harsh Cornish landscape in which he grew up.

Helen Keller at Wrentham

Two whip-poor-wills and five deer:
I was told about them and the symbols fitted.
My balcony rail had to vibrate with unheard song,
And my orchard had to be invaded,
For I refused the austere slab,
Alabama-graven, over each closed sense.
Tutors watched me and never guessed
Where the statue leapt alive
Or what the ghost suppressed.

Nest: a word that means spring, eggs,
Feathers: I've only touched some feathers
Of these small creatures. That pair
Were at mating crest—one fussy amid apple-spray,
The other perched on the wisteria
That rubbed the rail I gripped: I caught every note
Pulsing through vine-cord and metal
From his unseen exultant throat.
And his love-trills fed my warm spasms of trance
Till I woke in a rainy fall,
Kissed under our pines and apple-twigs:
I, the debarred freak, breathed a woman's vows.

Cows: the word our servant used
For buck, doe and fawns—wild marauders,
Yet so delicate, so graceful, we did not molest them
In the orchard one summer day.
I had touched antlers—strange bony fans
Or clipped twisted wings; I fancied them glide
Above the gentle bodies, harmless as a fleeced flock.
But when they had gone we found havoc—
Fruit-trees destroyed, the bark all ripped away.

Jack Clemo
182

Yes, it's a true allegory
Of my heart's enchanted wood;
That was the fate which my deity,
Who is not the orthodox one, permitted.
Something gashed me—antler or teeth;
I was stripped, and because no whip-poor-will,
Nor will of mine or any man's
Could tap the dream back, I took up vaudeville,
The Red Flag, many unpopular causes.
My lopped mission has done some good,
But I cannot help dark soundless victims
To nest-thrills I lack. I'll muse on brotherhood.

Jack Clemo
183

Affirmative Way

Razored by frost and thaw, a quarry rim
Collapsed one night, quite near my home.
A curved jut of spongy topsoil
Heavy with bush-clumps and a stone hedge,
Was slowly loosened, severed, poised
In a brief tremor of roots and boulder,
Then thundering, a horror of rock-splinter,
Earth-clots and mangled twigs, into the moon-fingered pit,
Taking half the road with it.

I looked next day at the gashed ground,
Sheer drop from the road's centre,
And at the deep zigzag cracks
Networked for yards around.
I felt baulked, deprived, as this road led,
To the ridge of downs, my favourite spot
For mystic musings at twilight.

I recalled the maxims of the negative school,
The trite line of condolence:
"The blind glimpse truths that sighted people miss;
The deaf hear subtler tongues astir within;
The paralysed thrill with a rarer bliss. . . ."
None of that patter here! I could see
What became of my only highway
When a quarry-face caved in.

The soul's road to divine wisdom
Passes so close to the sensuous quarry
That a maiming of the fertile ledge—
Loss of touch, sound, movement, colour,

Jack Clemo
184

Topple of beauty's thrust and chafe—
Tears half the road away,
Leaving the rest unsafe.

You cannot trust an intuition
Flashed merely as a compensation.
The insight, the forced dream,
The theory, which a cripple shapes
To train, sustain, explain himself,
Falls sterile and untested,
Making no bridge for brisk feet
Blundering where herd-perils teem.

"The diviner learns because he lacks,"
Say the glib pundits. Well, take the extreme—
Abelard's curb, the pale scar,
The hollow voice on the broken path.
Did the eunuch match a Luther's fiery vision?
A Patmore's delicate victory of grace?
Not for *them* a passion's cold aftermath.

I can trust only the intact road
Marking the pure unmutilated edge
Before the frost came, before the quarry-crust fell.
My creed was proved by keen sense-evidence—
Tossed tint, girlhood's frown and smile,
Bold scarps crossed by lusty horses;
And I still ignore the blockage, hearing
The old winds move above the riper seed-swell.

Jack Clemo
185

Whispers

These whispers must come from ahead,
From a point where the road bends round
Into faith-flushed terrain again,
Beyond the last factory-shed
Of secular mirage. They have haunted
Not merely my raw birth-dower
Of iron tracks, quarry-faces
And thin sand-scratching furze,
But palm and pebbly beach more fitly hers
Whose whisper warms, confirms their message.

To tire of current babble
Could not evoke such clear intimations
Unless something lived and moved, articulate
Outside the jarring circuit: without this,
My fret or boredom could bring only
The screwed frost of silence.

I am not tired: the whispers give me power,
Not insulating, sealing me in an archaic climate.
I have trudged the menaced and changeful way
Down through the twentieth century,
Smelt petrol, drugs and bleaching chemicals,
Passed super-markets, laboratories, clinics.

I have heard men's voices barking on the moon,
Bomb-clouts and the shrieked pop tune;
Stood under excavators that baptized me
With rain from their poised dull teeth;
Seen white spoil-heaps, first conical, turn oblong,
And subtler crusts of thought turn sour.

Jack Clemo
187

I know what today's paper claims
For the birth pill, what some bishops preach
About a shrivelled God and shrivelling morals,
And what young trendy poets write
Concerning urinals.
I have caught the dry jargon, watched the expert hands
Plaster neat labels on holy places,
Call the terrible secret of God a neurosis,
The terrible insights of sex an obsession.

The whispers that echo in my lines
Laugh gently among buds of the future,
For a wind will rise against the vulgar term,
And terror is truth in the intermediate
Regions between nullity and centre.

If flawed cells flared in the murmuring germ
Till I rasped and hurled rocks like a clay titan,
There is no regret on the lulled levels,
For they are private. The rebel's
Fire and peril remain; intense
Listening stiffens my rejection
Of the broad escape-route's signs.
Even her pebbly beach under the calm bran-
Coloured cliff borders the oolite quarries
Where stone was cracked to bear
A whispering gallery, like our faith's, ringed by nightmare.

Jack Clemo
188

Beethoven

Fate tuned him for the abysmal soundings
Through Bonn's wine-dense disguise:
In penury at raping sunrise
The wizard was adrift, tossing to keys and strings
Those flickers and pulsations—magnetism
Of wild inhuman currents working schism
In the flesh-dank shadow that slipped fast
Over the tavern songs, the shafted laughter
Of glutted harpies plying their noble birth
On his moody shallows of vanity.

There was too much pride, too much disdain
In the fluted bubbles, the sullen quivers,
The quick raging melody.
His hard face, held too high,
Grew clenched and masked in silent waterfalls:
An insatiate nerve was blocked from the feeding
Cascades of inns and gala-houses,
Forests and pastures and cathedral bells.

Turn aside, think of Norse sagas
Or Greek myths. There's an irony that appalls
Unbearably in his claustral striving.
A titan spirit writhes and cries
For the living test of its dumb symphonies,
While the discordant gods look down
With their cold star-stilling frown,
Ready to mock the last
Convulsion of the stricken heart
When rebellious strains have failed,
All shared rhythms snapped, embittering webs prevailed.

Jack Clemo
189

Wait till the *Kyrie* rises, then scan him again:
See his face soften, clear of fate's pouring web,
Laved with a glow of Luther's secret.
This is faith's music, purged of the long fret,
Moving to the *Gloria* which he can hear
Forestall, outlive the marginal ambush—
That final hush in which he lies
On a ragged bed in Vienna,
His numb fist shaken at the lightning-fleer.

Jack Clemo
190

Frances M. Parsons

Frances Margaret (Peggy) Parsons was born prematurely, and though she was not expected to live, she survived through the careful nurturing she received during the first crucial weeks of her life. She entered the California School for the Deaf in Berkeley in 1931 and later attended public schools, Gallaudet University, Howard University, George Washington University, and the University of Maryland. As a young teenager, Parsons lived in Tahiti, where she gained respect for other cultures. Combining this respect with her convictions about the culture and leadership capabilities of deaf people, she has worked toward acceptance of total communication throughout the world. Parsons works internationally with professionals who educate deaf children. She was instrumental in developing the Peace Corps's program for the deaf in the Philippines and served as the Peace Corps's first deaf participant-traveler in the Far East, Kenya, and Seychelles. Parsons has an M.A. in art history and was a faculty member at Gallaudet University for nineteen years. Currently, she is Coordinator of International History Collections at the Gallaudet library. She has received numerous awards, has appeared on "Nova" (PBS) and in *People* magazine, and has published extensively.

Selections from
I Didn't Hear the Dragon Roar

All my life I had dreamed of seeing China. The Cultural Revolution forced me to wait, but in the early 1980s I began taking steps to make my trip a reality. I intended to manage on a shoestring budget, something I was familiar and comfortable with. I had managed quite well when I traveled around the world this way in 1976. When I told my friends and colleagues of my plans, however, their enthusiasm was less than whole-hearted.

"Of course you must see China!" they said. Many added, "But it is far from an easy place to visit on your own under any circumstances. For a hearing-impaired woman like yourself, it will be impossible." The more knowledgeable advisers became alarmed when I mentioned that I hoped to find the cheapest lodging and transportation and did not plan to travel first class. They repeatedly warned me about the difficulties, hardships, and frustrations that lay ahead.

Many people believed that my hearing impairment would prove an insurmountable handicap. Probably their attitude strengthened my determination to travel independently. Certainly I am not above going out of my way to prove a point. I must also confess to being stubborn; stubbornness is a flaw in my character that I have developed to near perfection in my sixty-some years on this planet. But the most important consideration was one bare and unassailable truth. If I traveled first class or with a tour group, I could hardly afford to stay in China for six weeks. I would not be there long enough, and I would not travel far enough to see the country as I wanted, nor would I be able to visit schools for the deaf.

My hearing impairment is nothing new. I was born with

Frances M. Parsons
192

very little hearing, but I speak well enough for almost anyone to understand me most of the time. Once, when I was traveling around the world in 1976, some skeptics accused me of being a hearing person pretending to be deaf. I had to have my audiogram sent to me from home to prove that they were wrong.

My deafness did not prevent me from acquiring a career as an art historian when I was in my forties. A divorcee with two daughters in their teens, I earned a bachelor's degree at Gallaudet University. . . and afterward pursued graduate studies at the University of Maryland, Howard University, and George Washington University. At the same time, I began teaching courses in art history at Gallaudet.

My second career, a direct result of my hearing impairment, set me on the path that would eventually take me to China. It began in 1971, when a friend representing the Council of Organizations Serving the Deaf sent me to Argentina for the summer. There, sponsored by the government, I held seminars for teachers of deaf children and taught sign language to deaf adults. At one particular school I visited, I entered a classroom unannounced and found the children either sleeping on their desks or daydreaming while they waited their turns to practice speech. They had no books or paper work. The teacher, who held a pair of metal tongs, sat opposite a little girl. The teacher used the tongs to correct the child's pronunciation, twisting her tongue until she produced the correct sound. When the teacher got up to welcome me, the child turned, tired and dazed, toward me. I will never forget the look on her face. The sight changed my life. I felt that someone had to speak for deaf children who could not speak for themselves.

For years, I had heard good and bad things about Shanghai. The largest city in China, Shanghai . . . may be the empress of the East or the scandalous whore of the Orient, depending upon one's perspective. It was once a megalopolis overrun with pimps, prostitutes, child slaves, drug runners, foreigners, wealthy traders, and even university intellectuals. When the Party came to power in 1949, it sought to transform this city of contrasts, full of coolies and millionaires, into a showcase. The Communists demolished slums and tried to eradicate prostitution. They instituted housing projects, provided rehabilitation for opium addicts, and abolished child and slave labor. City traffic and transportation were improved—and many intellectuals were "persuaded" to go elsewhere. Unwanted infants of the destitute can no longer be found floating in the Yangtze, and the opium wars have ceased. The Communists succeeded where the missionaries had failed, but many tourists no longer find Shanghai worth visiting. Still, the city won my heart in the five days I spent there . . .

I was now suffering from a bronchial cough, an enlarged larynx, excruciating foot pain, and fever. Still I refused to go to bed. A porter who carried my bags to my dorm expressed concern and suggested that I take a taxi to a hospital, but my pocket was still smarting from the high taxi fare that I had paid to travel from the train station to the hotel. When I insisted on going by bus, he helpfully showed me to a bus stop three blocks away. My luck was beginning to change. I complimented the porter on his command of English, and he acknowledged my words with a charming smile. Self-taught, he apparently haunted bookstores, looking for English books and cassettes.

Getting off the bus at the Bund (an Anglo-Indian word for the embankment of a muddy waterfront, according to my guidebook), I sought help at the Peace Hotel in getting a taxi from there to the hospital. The first clerk asked with a big smile, "Which room?" When I shook my head, his smile faded, and he slammed the cradle on the phone, turning his back on me. The second clerk looked away, shamefaced. I stepped outside the front entrance and tried to hail three different taxis, but it was possible to get their attention only through the taxi service inside the hotel. The First People's Hospital was five blocks away. It took me half an hour to get there, alternately limping and sitting on the curb as passersby stared at me.

The foreigner's clinic was located on the sixth floor, and there was almost no privacy. Patients, alone or with a group of concerned family hovering nearby, waited while a doctor or nurse tended each person in turn either on a chair or on an examining table with a small, short screen beside it.

After a considerable time, Dr. Kung turned his attention to me. He did not smile. Small of stature, delicate, and bony in build, he seemed to concentrate all his strength in his face. I acknowledged my deafness and spoke about my problems. He started to speak, but I immediately asked him to write instead.

He stared. "But you can speak!" he protested.

I patiently explained that my ability to speak did not mean that I could hear or lipread.

He persisted, "But you speak too well!"

"I can speak. Can you *write?*" I replied.

We argued at some length, and I was so amused by his bewilderment that I began to tease him. When he made the mistake of writing in Chinese, I answered by signing. He broke into a smile.

On my last day in Shanghai, I slept later than usual and ambled three blocks to the first-class Shanghai Hotel, the only skyscraper, for a Western breakfast. I entered the lobby and gaped to see an American couple using American Sign Language! It turned out that a group from Herb Tours had arrived the night before. Herb Schreiber had been a friend of mine for forty years. Our paths had last crossed in Manila twelve years before, when he was leading his tour group and I was helping to found a total communication school for the deaf. I now had more than one reason to renew our acquaintance. For nearly two weeks I had been trying in vain to find the type of note pad I used to outline my journal. Herb, on the other hand, had just arrived from America—the land of plenty.

Crossing my fingers I asked, "Do you have a note pad with perforated pages?"

He not only had more than one but found he could part with three . . .

Taking my last walk along the riverbank, I saw a group of deaf Chinese adults signing under the scrutiny of an ever-larger crowd of curious bystanders. When the deaf people noticed me watching them, I smiled and signed in elementary Chinese. After that they wouldn't let me go for the next two hours and treated me to a restaurant meal that disagreed with me.

The question of how to sign "love" arose, but when I demonstrated the American sign, they were shocked, finding the hug in our sign too personal: to them it suggested spouses behind closed bedroom doors. They told me that during the Cultural Revolution most deaf people were spared extreme hardships and manual labor in the fields. One deaf person who stayed in America longer than the Communists liked was made an exception to the rule, however; he suffered agonizing torture. But these people also recalled that all of the deaf had been required to undergo acupuncture treatments. While acupuncture may help with many other problems, it is apparently no cure for most hearing impairments.

A hearing six-year-old grandson of one of the women signed, "America good. Here no good."

I explained that every country has both good and bad conditions, laws, and so on. His grandmother had avoided using sign language as a means of communication when she reared her hearing daughter. Now, realizing that she had made a mistake, she and her only grandson signed and fingerspelled all the time.

Delores Goodrick Beggs

Delores Goodrick Beggs is a prolific writer whose poetry and fiction have been published in anthologies and in numerous small press publications, including *Sunrust, American Pen Women, Pennsylvania Poetry Society Prize Poems, Pinehurst Journal, Facet,* and *Z Miscellaneous.* Recipient of a 1992 Artists Fellowship from the Arts Council of Santa Clara County, she is also the author of a collection of science fiction stories, *Myrfa C'an and the Edgestones and Other Skyhorse Stories,* and a nonfiction book, *How Can I Talk With You.* Beggs has been a small press columnist for the past three years, previously for *Guidelines Magazine* and *Writer's News and Markets,* and currently for *Midnight Zoo* and the soon-to-be-launched Experiences Unlimited Writer's and Artist's Organization marketing publication. Delores Goodrick Beggs has a severe hearing loss due to a childhood bout of spinal meningitis. She reads lips.

Tinnitus

It's more than just a lack
  of sound, you see,
mere silence wouldn't give me
  so much trouble!
It's insistent, undulating pressure,
  outside, sound pounding
on unyielding door
while inside, the broken doorbell's
  stuck on ring
like persistent phone crank
  gleefully redials,
and lets it ring, and ring;
until I want to scream
hang up, hang up! Can't you tell
  nobody's home?

Delores Goodrick Beggs

Christopher Heuer

Christopher Jon Heuer was born in 1970, in the small farming community of Hustisford, Wisconsin. Very early in his life, it was discovered that he was severely hard-of-hearing, probably because of genetic causes. Upon graduation from high school, Heuer entered the University of Wisconsin-Milwaukee as an English major. Now a third-year student, he plans to graduate in 1992 and go on to pursue an M.A. in philosophy at U.C.L.A.

Larynx

Deafness has broken my nose and my teeth
it has injected novocaine into my lips
my throat has been parched,
my tongue stiffened and disconnected.
I might as well drool on the rug
and shriek like a monkey
perhaps I could dress in flowing robes
and preach on Venice Beach.

This voice does not belong
behind a president's desk
it should mop the floors of morgues
and tidy-wipe urinals in public restrooms.
It is a voice for lethargic cannibals
and retarded Medieval executioners.

If these rabid hands possessed a blade,
I would shear an ear from the gaping bystander
so enthralled with my wicked arcs and swirls.
Perhaps at the sight of his own appendages
flopping on the sidewalk,
he might overlook the horrific octaves of my song
as I dance my way down the street
to its light vibrations.

Christopher Heuer
201

Howling at the Moon

We are all equal under the moon
you and I certainly are, at least
as we sit here and breathe it in
for neither of us can smell it
or taste it, though as romantics
we would like to think we can;
green cheese the furthest thought
from our minds as we do.
We cannot touch it yet
but our children might
and if you want to howl at it
I could join you if I wished.
And though my deafness makes
a difference under the sun that
illuminates our lives,
it is acceptable under the moon
where our business is finished
and there is only the need
to sit, like this, and stare.

Christopher Heuer

Spiraling into Sleep

We are eggshells
from hell
my friend, we are not immortal.

I'm afraid of how you look
under this Vaseline gook
that covers your face,

of your mangled cheek
and the strangled shriek
in your stuffed-deerhead eyes

as I examine where
you once had hair,
now a tube in a red welt,

a drain
for your brain
under more pressure than it ever was.

I wonder how it felt,
my friend, when you realized a belt
would have kept you among us
and out of the sleep
that you spiraled into, so deep-
ly, that you may never wake again.

I am waiting, my friend,
for you to awaken, and
I am praying that you will wake as yourself.

Christopher Heuer
204

Joseph Castronovo

Joseph Castronovo is a writer and performer of poetry in both English and American Sign Language. A very active force in deaf arts, he established the International Deaf Cultural Arts and Humanities/American Center, Inc.; was instrumental in starting the KUNST Academy for European Deaf artists and humanists; is a founder of the International Deaf Cultural Arts Academy (IDCAA), headquartered in Stockholm, Sweden; and was a founder of the Los Angeles First Deaf Visual Arts Exhibit. Castronovo has worked at the Los Angeles Music Center/Mark Taper Forum, where he helped with the development of the play, *Children of a Lesser God*. Born of deaf parents, he has three brothers and one sister, all of whom are hearing. Castronovo is now married to Graziella Anselmo of Italy and has two hearing daughters, Amaramini and Asavanimarei.

Statues

A Panegyric to the 18th Century French Deaf Leaders

I stood before a panoramic view
Of a rolling hill of green grass.
There was nothing else to see.
I asked myself,
> "Why am I here?"

As I strolled ahead
A sight appeared
> To my far left,
> many trees . . . and,   to my far right,
>> Many statues.

Silent, all in white,
As if running, hands outstretched to me.
Those transparent statues' souls
Overflowed with pain and sorrow.
They were deaf teachers.

Reaching out to one soul
I understood the plea:
> "Hurry! Hurry! Or you will be like us."
My heart, aching, responded:
> "Yes, I will."

Beyond the statues was the setting sun.
Reddish-orange in hue.
The grass blushed greener, yet
Something beckoned me forward.
I walked faster.

Feeling a sense of direction, I wondered,
> "What's the quest?"

Joseph Castronovo
206

A faint breeze allayed my frown;
If I accomplished the search
I would not see my hands rise likewise.

I arrived at a castle door, sealed.
And then, it was ajar;
A long pavement, with grass on both sides
Unfolded ahead of me.
I followed the course.

Now, another castle door of the inner court:
It was opened by a gentleman. He welcomed me
And indicated me to go on further.
Another long sidewalk directed my way:
The grass was still on both sides.

And then, a third door, the Chamber Door,
Unlocked to a small, dark foyer.
Behind the Door I was ushered
To an unseen stairway;
Its descent was long and spiral.

I beheld a view of a King's bedchamber,
Grey stone tiled.
Hanging torches lit the room.
Across from me, above the King's bed
A rectangular painting did suspend.

An essence of emotion:
The painting engrossed me.
Enticing me to come closer;
I found myself standing, left knee on the bed
Observing . . .

A mound of green grass;
        To my upper left,
        A clear blue sky . . . and, to my extreme right
                        A huge institution

Joseph Castronovo

Amazed as I was, the scene engulfed me.

Outside of a white fence, I stood watching
Deaf children playing within the barrier.
They wore red capes;
A chill crept over me. . .
        "The Cloak of Death."

Unaware children, now in pairs,
Danced into the main entrance of the edifice;
Above it in an alcove
Stood a white statue: armless!
I fled from the dreadful scene.

I was brought to the original setting, but where
The trees were to my left were now the statues.
As the sun was rapidly sinking,
I looked at my Parisian boots, saying. . .
        "I must surpass the statues."

So that other Deaf people alive today
Wouldn't hope in vain.
I raced for the sun.
The centuries-old statues
Vacuumed me in with them.
A statue, I too became.
My arms outstretched
Toward the fainting rays of the sun
Sunken!

I woke up.

Above the Entrance to an Ancient Italian Cemetery, a Sign

"Before we were like you, but later you will be like us"

In my sleep
Chants an old man in signs
"Those people lie in the dark!"

In my dream
Chants the old man in signs
"Go fetch the old book!"

In my rouse
Chants the old man in signs
"They shall rise!"

One summer afternoon in Florence
Its Biblioteca, its stale archives
Whispered into our hands the forbidden knowledge:

Published in 1834, "Come Maestri Sordi;"
Its awesome passages "renaiss-sane"
Italian Deaf people from the "1990 Dark Age."

"Tis the truth of this only remaining book"
Exclaimed as they scuffed their way
Into their Graves and Births.

Joseph Castronovo
209

Peter Cook

Peter Cook is a deaf performance artist who employs elements of mime, storytelling, acting, and poetry. He is codirector and founder of Flying Words Project, a nonprofit literary organization that promotes literature in American Sign Language. Cook has performed throughout North America, including the Cleveland Performing Arts Festival, Friends and Artists Theatre in Los Angeles, Manhattan Theatre Club, and the Whitney Museum of American Art. His work has been reviewed by the *L.A. Times, High Performance,* and the *Boston Globe,* and was the pick-of-the-week in the *Village Voice* and *Dramalogue.* Cook has made television appearances on "Live from Off Center" (PBS), "Poetry Spot" (WNYC) and "Off Hand" (Silent Network). He currently lives in Chicago.

Maltz

I asked the old man with a cane
what was in his black bag.
with his eyes on his watches, he sign:
two books.
what books, I sign.

one a spy novel
two The Three Musketeers
And came up with third question: why?

He looked at me in a silence for four seconds.

    I wanted to die with a clear image of
    The musketeers eating their boar's tongue
    while their tips of swords drinking
    the blood of the enemies as
    their home being raped by a fire of cannon balls
    and the sound of fat ladies' giggles.

Ringoes

Only thing I could remember was
smell of August humid tall grasses in
beam of the afternoon sun.
It was sunday.
I knew it because I did not have to sit
on the pew and play tic, tac, and toe with my dad.

Ron was the only boy I could play with
because God have all angels on this days.
and I did not feel bad.

I knew God watch them in their mon-sat mischief

Ron, reach out for my shoulder

tap

tap

tap

As I turn around,

Ron's teeth seemed to close tight and smile
without raising his eyebrows.
His teeth wide opened and I could see his tongue
touched the frontal teeth, then snapped back to the
back of his mouth, and his apple in his turtleneck
sweater shook rapidly.

Only thing I understand was fear in his eyes.

Peter Cook
212

I focused on where his path of eyes
aimed at:
Three crawling garter snakes
acting as climbing vines among
tall grasses of my own backyard.

A mind editing image flashed in my head;
a teacher holding a picture card of a green snake
next to her mouth.
She did what Ron did to me:

> SSS NAAEE K

She pointed at the picture.
She did again what Ron did to me:

> SSS NAAEE K

She did repeat with the picture until I become her
dog: I nodded my head.

All I know that snakes have tiny tongues
but what it got have do with ss naaee k?

Hannah Merker

Hannah Merker's first story was published in a local newspaper when she was ten. Since then, she has published in hundreds of newspapers, journals, and anthologies, including *The New York Times,* the *Chicago Tribune,* and *The Christian Science Monitor.* After years of simultaneous careers as a librarian and university teacher, and what she calls "seven wonderful years" of owning her own bookshop, Merker now devotes her time to writing. Merker lives on a houseboat with her husband, five cats, and a hearing ear dog.

Selections from Listening

At a certain point you say to the woods, to the sea, to the mountains, the world, Now I am ready. Now I will stop and be wholly attentive. You empty yourself and wait, listening . . . you wait, you give your life's length to listening. . . .

Annie Dillard, *Teaching a Stone to Talk*

The world stands still where we are. And that small piece of planet is ours alone. However cluttered in crowds of colleagues and comrades, families, friends, we each receive the messages of earth, and respond to them, from our separate stance.

Sometimes the messages are unclear. Sometimes we do not receive them at all and so do not respond.

How can you know that the world around me is quiet, that I do not hear your step behind me, or hear you call my name from a distance? The silence around me is invisible. How can you know that the songs of new birds in spring, the crunch of old leaves, the soft sigh of the west wind, all subtle sounds that color the day for you, are not there for me? The whir of a car, the pounding feet of a runner behind us as we walk, the soft slap of rain on a roof, are so elementary a part of your perceptions you cannot imagine that for a person at your side they may not exist. How can you know unless I tell you?

And how can I tell you about something that is not there, if part of my mind is asleep, no longer associates sound with a particular circumstance?

So, then, we must talk to each other, listening in our own ways. Perhaps, while walking with me on the beach, or on some sandy shore-side path, you will ask yourself, "What do I hear at this moment?"

Hannah Merker
215

Perhaps you will touch my arm, so that I will look at you, and you will say, "The wind is whispering in the willow trees," or "The gulls, there, are screeching over the fishing nets," or "Someone nearby is playing a violin."

I still will not hear these things, but now I will know they are there, perhaps remember that once I knew without conscious thought that sound is connected to the swaying willow, the gull. The world becomes larger as the mind reawakens to the soaring symphony of everyday life. We have both forgotten these sounds are there.

And so this book is about listening—about new ways of listening for the hearing and the hearing impaired.

And it is about a brave experiment that risked a great friendship, an experiment that kindled an augmenting ongoing adventure for me, at this still place in the world where I stand.

I like to watch him . . . I know where he stands and where his voice goes on the rolling grasses and where the sun comes up on the land. There, at dawn, you can feel the silence. It is cold and clear and deep like water. It takes hold of you and will not let you go.

N. Scott Momaday, *The Way to Rainy Mountain*

He sat on the top step of the companionway, blinking away rain dripping from the hood of his foul weather jacket, waiting for my full attention, smiling, musing abstractions appearing as creases above his eyes. "How can I tell you the sound of the foghorn," he said, "describe how I hear night rain on the deck, on the dock, on the melting ice?"

I touched his hand, a silent gesture to convey the wave of

caring that came over me, an unspoken "thank you" for giving a piece of the soft evening to me, for reminding me of the forgotten part of it that was there, the part I cannot hear.

"You have just told me," I said, and he knew memory was struggling to some shadowy recess trying to remember a foghorn rising and receding on a reachable horizon, the dull drone of a deep sigh over invisible water, gentle and firm, a giant's voice guarding the near breakwater, reaching out from those rocks every seven seconds in an ascending arc, leaving only a mind echo.

He stood then at the foot of the stairs, the open hatch above his head letting in the rain, the remarkable sky. We had noticed it earlier, walking our dog. Clouds scudded swiftly, grays and lavenders disappearing in gathering night mist. Through the hatch I could see a ribbon of white curling in a light south wind, steam from the garbage-burning plant down the inlet, wispy then lost in a vanished fog-world.

"Maybe," he said, "the foghorn is a sound not unlike an open G string." He smiled, hopeful. I tried to recall the rich tone of a violin's lowest string unstopped by fingers, a plucked evocation of a rising and falling of vibrating air. Once I knew the foghorn, the G string.

"And the rain." He turned, sliding shut the hatch, slipping off the wet slicker, tossing it over a door to dry. "How can I describe how beautiful it is?"

"It is light," I say, almost to myself, "almost a whisper . . . sinking silently into the wood of the dock, perhaps plinking off our deck, merging into the melting ice." I know the plinking on deck must be muted, faint, even restful, a surprise with the soft air of this mid-February evening. I know the rain. We have talked about rain before. It is the foghorn we have forgotten to remember.

The foghorn becomes a small miracle, then an infinite wonder as we try to make tangible its essence, its august statement, mournful and solemn: I am rocks, I am ship, I am presence, I am here with you though you cannot see me. And the sound becomes anthropomorphic, as do many sounds, as we talk about them. They become alive to me in ways they never were when I could hear them.

"Tonight's rain," Harvey says to me, "is like this." He brushes my face with light glancing kisses, lips just resting on cheeks, eyes, lips, then gone, leaving a moist sweetness. I know what rain is like tonight, a tenderness I can guess from walking in it, touching it, but now I think I know its other dimension, can almost "hear" its sound, tonight close to silence.

My world—the world I know—is hushed, a happening from a skiing accident more than twenty years ago. One morning the world was there, perceived as it was every other morning, without conscious thought about what I saw, what I heard. By evening of that day the world I knew had changed, one dimension of perception dimming, soon nearly disappearing, the colorful sequence of words and sounds eclipsed until, months later, I almost forgot those chromatic cadences had ever been there.

Almost.

Memory was there, waiting for me to prod it, poke at its intricate filing system, play with its stored reserve of subtleties. Memory was motionless holding its breath, waiting to be prompted, waiting for urgency to invoke recall, the remembrance of sound. Memory waited for me to use it. What I needed, though I did not know it yet, was to learn a new language, to limn the linguistics of visual and auditory cues that were everywhere, there for me but unnoticed, unseen, unheard. I needed to learn the language of listening. Can there be such a thing—a listening language—a linguistic composite capturing the complexity of thought and quest, catching the nuances of conceptual thinking, of feeling, of mood that can be found in, say the Italian language, the French, the Hebrew, or in Sign, that exquisite choreography of silent movement and expression and fluttering fingers?

Indeed, Sign *is* a listening language, depending on visual attention and interpretation, a means of linguistic communication with a structure comparable to written and spoken languages. The many sign languages, all with individual forms of grammar and sentence structure, some including gestures of hand, head, and body to articulate the intent of meaning, are as real living languages as any written or spoken cultural cumulation of verbal expression. The hearing impaired, the not-totally deaf who have once known hearing and speech, often incorporate if not the syntax, then some of the physical means used by sign languages to both impart and receive communication.

As an adult losing most of my hearing suddenly, a loss leaving me in a strange semi-silent place, was a state akin to being adrift in a fog where the edges of nearby land, and other fog-bound craft, are barely visible. You know something is there but definition is vague. Depth perception plays tricks with distance. You miss a lot, the fog hiding much in a moist mist, sometimes unexpectedly lifting, giving you a glimpse of something you cannot make out. No one knows you are lost for you look the same. You can speak clearly the language you have known for years, but now your own voice and the voices of others are muffled, muted, or not there at all. You are aware, yet cut off, alone in a scary isolation. The world is running forward and you cannot keep up. That is what it is like to be severely hearing impaired.

Who teaches the language of listening, and can it be taught? Not at all surprising is that my first teacher was a dog—my devoted brindle boxer—the first to recognize that I needed other ears, for though memory was ready, willing to supply years of gathered information, it needed to know where to focus its research. We are information collectors, though we may never think of ourselves that way. Everything we do and see and hear and read, all the people we meet, all the worlds we touch are recorded in the library stacks of our minds. So much is there waiting for the right buttons to be pressed. You notice this most in doing crossword puzzles, especially sitting down to one that looks impossible from the first. You get a letter here, a word there, then suddenly memory clicks. Of course! You knew that all along! Just needed a reminder, a jolt, a trigger to awaken the slumbering tidbit stored there who knows when.

It is there, the world, its music, its noise, its voice. I am in touch with it through the ears of others and my own memory of what has sound attached to it. Two hearing aids make more words recognizable to me but hearing aids are limited (in this early stage of their evolution) in the magic they can perform. More than my hearing aids, I need Harvey and Sheena, I need my sisters, my friends, all partners with me in listening.

"It's alarming," Harvey murmurs, an inert form beside me, unmoving although he has a commuter train to catch to New York. I cannot hear the alarm, a modernness that beeps more than alarms, Harvey tells me. Memory has not stored the sound of beeping alarm clocks for me. They have come into the world after my deafness. So each morning when Harvey mutters "it's alarming" I think of the round white-faced clock with large, black numbers that jangled me alive eons ago, always at an hour, it seemed, before I was ready to face the world. Harvey stretches, sits up, careful not to disturb the cat, or two or three, sharing our bed. I close my eyes against sound waves I know are present, happy they are hidden from me. My life is improved without alarm clocks. Alarms of the alarming kind, that is, those of strident sound, those of an insistent signal signifying morning, symbolic sonic statements spinning through the silence of sleep, violent disruptions of a natural kind of order. I have a different kind of awakening clock.

No mechanical messenger brings morning's coming to me. I have an alive, alert, attentive presence, rousing herself from her own repose to tell me night is leaving, that light is creeping over the eastern sky. Sheena, my canine ears, is trained among other things to be an alarm clock, to awaken without being alarming, to whisk me gently from the warmth of woolen blankets, wing me away from the weight of sleep.

Sheena knows our routine. She is stretched where she has been sleeping on a small settee adjacent to our bed. She watches Harvey sleepily stumble by our coal stove to the beeping loran-alarm clock, watches him press a button erasing the sound for those who can hear it. Her ears, her eyes follow him. He has walked the four or five steps into our galley, filled the copper kettle with cold water. Sheena lifts an ear, an acknowledgement not only of the splash of water into the empty drum of the kettle, but also of the electrical hammer-like pounding of our water pump, a low guttural grinding of gears that accompanies the turning on of our faucets. If I am alert enough, watching her, struggling to stretch my eyelids against their slumbering intent, I will see the lift of her other ear. Harvey is grinding beans for our morning coffee. In my near-slumber, in the snug cocoon of my bed, half aware of beginning day, I am listening to morning, hearing it without sound, knowing it all by cues from listening ears, ears that are not my own.

I resist the moment of change from warmth to cold air. Harvey has not yet attacked the fire. No abrasiveness yet assails the dim light, the sound of shaking down the night's ashes, a sound I will know is there when I see him sitting on the step by the stove, shivering while he plays with the morning fire, coaxing it back to vibrant life. The fire, too, has rested through the night, burning low in the early hours, needing the alarm of a shake and fresh fuel. I do not move, buried beneath the covers to my nose, until my personal alarm clock rings.

She is silent, setting about her work with no jarring to the senses. I sometimes think my first sense of her is a seductive dream I am still part of. Sheena begins with the part of me nearest the edge of the bed—an arm draped over the side, an elbow jutting over her settee—or if I am too cuddled under, my nose, my cheek, my forehead. I feel a rough tongue, an insistent paw pressing a hip, a shoulder, my hair. She does this only for a moment, her whole self expectant, waiting, giving me time. She knows me.

"Hmmmm. . ." I murmur, burrowing deeper under the blankets. Instantly Sheena is on the bed, a gentle but firm emphatic presence, two paws on my shoulders, a nose nuzzling my neck. "Get up," she is saying, "coffee is ready, morning is here, you love mornings."

And I do. Love mornings, that is. I am always resistent to rising, yet happy to be up, eager to climb on deck, even when freezing, to watch the sun rise over the hills of Sea Cliff, over the hazy housetops of Glen Cove, over the incinerator stack not far from us at the head of the creek. Sheena is a superior alarm clock even if a silent one. She will not be ignored or turned off until obeyed. She persists, knowing I relish the early hours.

In the half-light, half-dark we sit in the enclosed cockpit of our home, the good ship Haimish, sipping strong coffee, a fresh-ground blend of espresso and French roast beans, the mixing, the smelling, the sipping all making a miracle of our mornings.

A gesture does not exist alone in time.
                    Martha Graham

It is late April and they are here every morning now, the
ménage à trois (sometimes quatre ou cinq), mama resplendent
in cinnamon and puce, ecru and umber (what the books so
unimaginatively call mottled brown). She waits for me on the
substructure of the dock to which our floating home is tied,
sitting on beginning gatherings of grass and twigs and down
carefully placed on the boards she has nested on for years.
Her drake pulses a shiny green-purplish head a few feet from
my window, Broken Wing and other challenging rogues seemingly still in a respectfully distanced arc behind him. Not for
long.

My morning appearance, when it happens, initiates movement. In my old bathrobe, still foggy with sleep, I am light
years away from them in garb and attention. My left hand
reaches for the mug of steaming black coffee Harvey places
before me. My right hand automatically unlatches the window,
pushing it open. I have not called to them as I will later in the
day when I feel more alive. I have just appeared at the window's edge. Only air and water are between us. Even as I
reach to the shelf behind me for the loaf of bread that is
always there, a fluttering has begun. Mallards and geese swim
toward me from the opposite shore of the creek, a gentle
wake rippling behind each bird. Black-headed gulls hover low
overhead, waiting to dive, to pluck a chunk of whole wheat
from the water. And papa duck lowers his head, flattens his
wings tightly against himself, becomes a speeding, brilliant
bullet aiming himself at the rogues who scatter and return.
"Movement," professed Martha Graham, "is the one speech
which cannot lie."

Papa mallard treads water a few feet from me, glancing
hither and yon protectively. No matter how many small
chunks of bread I toss out he will not take a bite until mama

begins to eat. I wait for her, tossing further to Broken Wing and the others. Mama does not like this, a swishing volcano-burst of energy from under the dock, vaulting the six or more feet from water surface to my eye level, white tail aquiver, flashing her dazzling blue speculum sides before settling in the water, rising once again, her whole self a vertical vibrating voice. Ah yes. "A gesture does not exist alone in time."

Aristotle believed perception, sensing and some under-standing of the immediate environment, was a characteristic of all animals and quite a few plants. Perceiving, he deduced, caused a physiological change in the perceiver, became part of memory. Therefore, biological studies, especially considera-tions of the senses, could not be separated from study of the mind. Last week, more than 2000 years after Aristotle, I read about a new discovery: "plant communities may be abuzz with conversations no one can hear" (Science News, March 23, 1991, p. 188). My pansies and petunias (and who knows what else) are staking out territory by underground signals, by "root communication." Oh, dear. What are my dill and parsley and thyme saying to each other? (She spends too much time at the typewriter, forgetting to water us!) Apparently plants send out wordless messages through their roots, chemical signals called allelopathy. Not so new. In 1880 Charles Darwin wrote a book (*The Power and Movement of Plants*) describing his reflections and observations of plant tendrils, their selective responses to stimuli, their elaborate movements that evince remarkable sen-sitivity to the provocations around them.

So it is. Communication is everywhere. A root wiggles, say-ing, this is my place. Mama mallard ejects herself skyward to my eye level, saying, Breakfast! (or lunch, or snack, or dinner, as the case may be). As soon as she begins to munch, papa may take a nibble, all the while wary of predators who want both breakfast and mama duck. He nibbles, then swivels, hunching down, zooming like a high-speed motorboat, a mis-sile aimed first at Broken Wing (who can easily outdistance him—he's the fastest duck on the creek), then at the other rogue ducks. While papa scoots at the others, Broken Wing takes a momentary sexual interlude atop mama. Breakfast.

Silent signaling is not just reserved for breakfast. An egg lingering lethargically somewhere along the female reproductive system can, at any time of day or night, according to recent research, exhibit selectivity, emitting a chemical lure, beckoning to particular potential partners among the perhaps 280 million sperm swimming her way from one ejaculation. Endocrinologists are at work trying to characterize and isolate the attractant.

Will the creation of a child cease to be, sometime in the future, a random miracle? Will there be any mysteries left? Is the best communication silent, wordless?

Could be. Nevertheless, I turn to Harvey, push aside my coffee, the toast and jam, use words. "Let's have breakfast . . ."

"You must watch her," Elsa said to me ten years ago, when Sheena became part of my life. "Watch the shape of each movement, how much effort is involved. Effort shape," Elsa said, leading Sheena in a mad-paced series of twirling leaps and jumps around her studio, "is the action, attempted endeavor [effort] that takes place in energy." Elsa recognized that although Sheena came to me superbly trained, she always would be adding to her canine nonverbal vocabulary. To become half of a successful team I must advert to every subtle stir of her silent silhouette.

My perceptions sharpened quickly. Elsa saw to that. Elsa, a dancer trained at Balanchine's School of American Ballet, made nonverbal communication clear to me by teaching Sheena to dance, sometimes on point (a slight leap of the imagination). To this day (oddly—poor publicity, I suppose) Sheena is Elsa's only four-footed student.

Anyone who has ever lived with animals is aware of unspoken indications of mood. What I knew from living with a continually changing population of dogs and cats (and uninvited, yet resident mice, spiders, ants) was not superficial. It was just not enough. Much of my understanding of the fluctuating feelings of my creatures depended on sound. Now sound had escaped me, still there but elusive, beyond my knowing. I needed to hone visual skills. I needed to really begin to see.

I watched her dance. Hardly Balanchine material, but then Elsa had worked miracles before. Our lessons were unscheduled, impromptu visitations at Elsa's studio when a class was in session. Sheena and I would climb the stairs, Sheena pausing midway, looking at me, her right ear lifted straight up, her head tilted sideways to the left, glancing upward, then at me, then upward again. After a while I knew this meant music. Elsa's class was practicing enchainements or classical ballet variations, watching form and stance in the mirrored wall opposite the studio entrance.

I never think of Sheena's lack of oral communication in our life together. (Her high sharp barks, her low guttural growls, are there for anyone else.) I am instead amazed by her ears that not only take in and translate sound for me but also seem to have a life of their own. Hardly a new perception. Darwin discussed this at length in *The Expression of the Emotions in Man and Animals*. "The ears," he wrote, "through their movements are highly expressive in many animals; but in some, such as man, the higher apes, and many ruminants, they fail in this respect. A slight difference in position serves to express in the plainest manner a different state of mind, as we may daily see in the dog. . . ." This is clear in Sheena's manner of telling me her water bowl is empty. She rushes to me with both ears pointed high—her signal for alarm—then drops her ears flat against her head, glances at the bowl that she has turned upside down, and runs to it, pushing it with an annoyed paw, rushing back to me, ears still plastered against her collie-like skull.

Hannah Merker
227

At Elsa's doorway, Sheena pauses an infinitesimal moment. I drop her leash. All grace is lost as she plunges toward Elsa, a tremolo rush of orange skidding to stillness at Elsa's toes, obeying Elsa's signal to her—a lifted hand, pointed finger raised, quickly lowered—meaning sit. Just as swiftly, Elsa raises an arched arm, hand bent downward at the wrist, moving one finger in a continuing upward spiral. Sheena swivels on hind legs in a remarkably unBalanchine attempt at a pirouette.

Ten years later. Sheena is not a dancer. And yes, she is, in the sense that she and I have learned that movement, overt signs of physical expression are indicative of more than the mere action; movement concerns the psyche as well, illustrates and conveys feeling, thinking. Effort shape comes to mean the outer visualization of an inner surge, manifest. What is necessary for the observer is acute consideration of the motion performed. A Labanotationist skilled in the system of recording movement in Dance defined such observation: "Behind each motion lies the inner originating impulse to which we give the name effort. Every action, from a tiny shiver to a jumping out of the way of an oncoming car, originates in some effort by the individual. In daily life, we complete our various jobs and express ourselves in various ways through a series of effort patterns."

I watch her dance. No plié, no pas de cheval, no grand leap can say more than the intricacies of Sheena's daily sign-dances to me. Again I think of Martha Graham: "The dance must be strong. All that is important is this one moment in movement. Make the moment vital and worth living. Do not let it slip away unnoticed and unused."

I watch her dance. Walk. Run. Speak to me in her sign-movement way, exploring with intelligence, conveying with care, our world. And I am struck, feeling her napping weight across my toes this moment as I sit at my typewriter. She is eleven years old, perchance more. A senior citizen of dogdom. I reach down stroking her rugged flank, reassuring myself of her presence. She rolls over on her back, lifting paws.

Of course. She prefers belly rubs.

He knew language in a way that I never will. He danced it from his soul. To him language was a mantle, wearable. To Momma, language was tenderness, a protective touch, a means to tell me her stories, to hold me close to her life. And together, they brought me to a language beyond signed words.

Ruth Sidransky, *In Silence (1990)*

A hand hovers hesitantly before my face, fingers fanning its far reaches before resting on my cheeks, my neck, my vocal cords, a thumb light, listening on my lips. It is the signal for me to begin our conversation. Receptive now to every flickering vibration, motion, breath, he smiles.

We speak to each other. Our random thoughts and feelings are perceived by this man through his fingertips; by me, by watching his lips. He cannot see me. He cannot hear me. Deaf and blind, he interprets speech through vibrations and lip movements, aware through sensory messages of the subtle nuances occurring in verbal exchange. He is listening. His voice is heard by me by tones still taken in by my inner ear, vague cadences caught, mute and muffled as they are, and by concentration on the vivid expressions of his face, his lips. We listen to each other, a conversation almost totally dependent on visual and tactile cues.

Dr. Robert J. Smithdas, Director of the Helen Keller National Center for Deaf-Blind Youths and Adults, is fluent in several languages. He is using three almost simultaneously at this moment. One is the Tadoma method of speech communication—a method developed by a teacher trying to convey communication skills to two deaf-blind students, Tad and Oma. In this method, the person without sight and sound "reads" the vibrations of a voice with the fingers, senses the position of the tongue, the movements of cheek hollows, the windpipe's airflow, all the large and small, swift or slow movements of muscles occurring with articulation. Bob is also using finger-spelling, the one-hand manual alphabet that relays words and letters. His left hand rests atop his secretary's hand, receiving by touch a series of finger and knuckle positions conveying the key words I am uttering; and third, Bob, though he cannot hear his own voice, is using speech.

He is a sought-after lecturer astonishing audiences with his resonant voice, his vocabulary, his irrepressible humor. Watching him, listening to him, it is easy to forget the separateness of his world. With a laugh, he is quick to remind you. Once years ago I asked him how he had learned to speak so well. Steadfastly, he said, he practiced articulation and deliverance with a friend, a blind opera singer. He remembers his first speaking engagement, the warm response of the audience, the loud applause he "heard" through the vibrations beneath his feet. He remembers the sound ebbing even as someone fingerspelled into his hand a bit of advice: next time it might be interesting to face the audience.

Bob's conversation is filled with sensory images: "I had been playing by myself, chasing June bugs and butterflies," he mused, remembering the day at the age of five when he became ill with spinal meningitis. "I recall to this hour the large gray cat with yellow eyes stretched out lazily on a porch across the street. Mother called me for lunch, hands on hips. She wore a bright print dress, her brown hair swept backward over her head." He recalls three months later "trying to erase the film of drowsiness that clung to me like a mist. The darkness was neither black nor gray, but a thick muddy fog." His own voice had become a babbling sound. He could not understand it, soon would not hear it at all. And he was blind.

Hannah Merker
230

Later, after a tour of the Helen Keller Center, I walk by myself through the halls. There are different colors at every intersection, the walls different textures. I close my eyes, walking slowly, fingers following the finite reaches of each texture, finding one, then another, feet feeling changes when one kind of tile changes to another, physically absorbing the impact of this special place. It is peaceful. It is beautiful, wholly uninstitutional. The outer grounds too are abloom with texture and color. I remember a section of Bob's autobiography *Life at My Fingertips* describing his first few months at Perkins Institute in Massachusetts: "I became familiar with the grounds. It had been a principle with the founders of Perkins that the unseeing and unhearing should live in an aesthetically inspiring environment, for beauty has its own channels of communication, even when the senses are deficient . . . the old chestnut in front of Tompkins Hall broke into blossom, its wonderfully flowering branches overhanging the low wall that ran along the campus . . . when I walked along the flagstone paths of the herb garden, my footsteps crushed leaves of thyme and sorrel, sending up a curtain of tart, mingled fragrances that hung like a giant censer in the sunlit air . . . and . . . I grew especially fond of a magnolia tree in the director's garden. . . ."

I opened my eyes and turned off my hearing aids. Morning sun lit an empty classroom looking out on a small garden. The room was long, an open door at either end. I sat down at a desk, my back to both doors, gazing out at the garden, taking notes on the morning.

I do not know how long I was there. Or how long they were there. It was when I dropped my pencil, watched it roll under another desk, reached for it, glancing up toward the door at the far end of the room that I saw them, talking to each other, each with fingers on the other's lips, free hands folded under and over each other's in fingerspelling, the sightless eyes of each gazing at some inner vision off in space, yet entirely together. I was breathless. It was beautiful. Bob

Smithdas and his deaf-blind wife Michelle, a teacher at the Center, catching a private moment together. And they did not know I was there. I was the tree falling in the forest.